EMOTIONAL INTELLIGENCE

The ultimate guide to master relationships, develop
your social skills and increase your E.Q. for a better life

Al Navarro

Table of contents

INTRODUCTION

Make an effort to think about the way you felt that the last time that your feelings ran. Are you currently on top of earth riding a blissful tide of euphoria? Or were you presently fighting with the impulse to rearrange everything on the room by throwing it around into a fit of anger? Irrespective of what the scenario might be, our minds are hard-wired to reevaluate our fair idea and only our emotions. This is the reason why understanding your emotions is essential to your perception of wellness.

What are emotions?

It works like that; what we see, hear, smell, taste, and touch move through us at the kind of electric signs, moving from cell to cell until finally attaining our brains. They proceed through the bottom of their mind, near the spinal column, before achieving the frontal lobe, the location where all that, clear, logical thinking can happen.

The one issue? These signs must move across the limbic system (the location where feelings have been created) until they can accomplish your logical, clear led frontal lobe. Which usually means that what we feel, what we see, hear, taste, smell, and signature, is experienced before it's experienced logically.

This is not a terrible thing. It has our emotions, in conjunction together with all our logical thought, that has enabled people to evolve and thrive exactly how we now have. With no emotions, with no perceptions of anger, anxiety, joy, despair, and pity (our five heart emotions) we might well not have left it this way as a species." the issue lies inside an inability a lot of people have by allowing our mental and logical wisdom to convey effortlessly.

EI, or emotional intelligence, to put it differently, is the ones ability to comprehend and interrogate one's emotions in addition to the feelings of other people. If you would like to make an impression on the favor of somebody, you must first acquire over her or his or his feelings. This is the reason why great women and men, present and past, are ready to do what that they perform; they also will have significant comprehension in these emotions and the way they relate with and allure to people. Emotional intelligence is unquestionably the most powerful force driving personal and social success.

EI is divided up into two categories that all have two subcategories. You've got:

· personal competence, composed of self-awareness and self-management.

· social competence, composed of societal consciousness and connection management

Self-awareness can be the knowledge of yourself and what makes you tick. It's the capacity to identify exactly what you separately want for the emotional and psychological equilibrium. Self-management, to put it differently, is the capacity to perform or never do to yourself. It's the power to put aside momentary gratification in the quest for long-term satisfaction, to specify what's going to provide you satisfaction in life along with your decisiveness in moving after it. Both of these faculties are what make your awareness of personal proficiency.

Social awareness is the power to grab on different people's feelings and comprehend what the driving force in it is. It's set by your capability to listen and observe, to comprehend others are thinking and sense even though you're not feeling the same way. Your awareness of societal awareness is directly linked with your ability to others. Dating direction can be the power to utilize your comprehension of the other emotions concerning your personal to navigate connections with people ardently. This will guarantee clear communication and efficient handling of battle. Both of these faculties are what make your awareness of social proficiency.

In a nutshell, is that the cornerstone of e.q.. In part, we'll dive deeper to how you can put these theories to training to not just effortlessly manage and establish a much better, fitter, more stable partnership on your own, however together with people around you also.

Even though a relatively new topic of analysis, psychology has been strongly recognized as an academic field and also widely educated in universities and frequently introduced into next degree students worldwide. Yet students are usually astonished to find out there is considerable ongoing debate concerning how psychology needs to be defined and just what the content and nature of analysis within this field ought to be. Specifically, there's a lot of disagreement concerning if psychology ought to be thought of a genuine science similar such as to chemistry or mathematics, or needs to be thought of as social science and science tasked with subjects like sociology. Researchers took varying positions connected for the disagreement predicated on a range of factors including, but not restricted by, the particular region of analysis or subdiscipline inside the subject of psychology, which is being researched, in addition to other tangible cultural and social facets. A comprehensive discussion with this disagreement is beyond the remit of the text. But what ought to be evident is that answering the question of what's psychology?'" is maybe not as straightforward as you can imagine and this particular question, even as we will notice, is specially related to this analysis of intellect. For that reason, chapter one begins with a succinct discussion of the problem; after that, a succinct history of mental intelligence is going to be supplied. The 2nd element of the chapter summarizes and summarizes a number of the main issues and disagreements concerning the area and an outline of the main evaluations of emotional intelligence which can be mostly now utilized in research and research is going to be given. All in all, the principal point of this phase is to offer a good base, especially for people that might not be knowledgeable about the area of mental intelligence. Once this was successfully achieved, readers will probably be armed with most the data and information that they might need to allow them to specifically explore how growing social and emotional skills may help students and teachers in a diverse learning environment.

Fundamental questions and issues arise as a result of this very various impacts that doctrine and physiology experienced over the creation of psychology. By way of instance, in the simplest level of enquiry, human behavior is observable and relatively readily listed and measured, whereas human experience is both subjective and not as readily accessible to scientific dimension (psychologists can view the naked eye the best way to act but may not readily know what it is that you 'feel'). Which usually means that specialists from the early years of research within the sphere of psychology, experience has been frequently considered more amenable to scientific investigation compared to behavior. The matter is very related to this main topic of mental intelligence because while intellect, the capacity to conclude was and is, quantified via monitoring or standardized tests, emotion isn't easily measured. Because of this, it's not surprising that artificial intelligence (IQ) has chiefly been concerning cognitive abilities like cognitive expertise, problem-solving and abstract and concrete reasoning that can be areas which are conducive to measurement. The measurement and comparison of such emotional abilities are knas 'psychometrics' and while areas like personality may also be evaluated psychometrically, an average of this field centers around measuring cognitive reasoning abilities. There's undoubted significance in doing this. Once confirmed individual, or real people's, it is understood, comparisons might be manufactured which can empower assistance and aid to be provided for people that might take it. Otherwise, psychometric testing can determine people that possess superior cognitive abilities. From a single perspective, psychometric testing helps increase self-knowledge by permitting you to recognize personal cognitive strengths which could possibly be capitalized upon and flaws which could possibly be addressed. The clearest benefit of this is in regards to career choice. Psychometric testing might help you to select a career path coordinated with key advantages, that will be naturally of significance not just to the average person but in addition to companies, teachers and possibly society altogether. An effective body of knowledge has been gathered that certainly shows the validity and equilibrium of psychometric dimension, and it has likewise confirmed a confident relationship between high IQ and academic achievement. There's definitely much significance in measuring student's IQ and in using this awareness to help encourage students within thEIr learning. But in modern times, many professors and researchers have discovered a sensed over-reliance on the dimension of IQ in academic settings.

CHAPTER ONE

EMOTIONAL INTELLIGENCE MODELS

Emotional intelligence is Your Ability to understand, comprehend, and take care of your emotions as well as the emotions of others in favorable ways. Now we can note bEIng "book smart" and using a top intelligence quotient, or IQ will not guarantee a more fruitful, joyful and satisfying life. There are various people in every section of the world that are rather brilliant academically but are somewhat furious at handling people and power in the office or within their relationships. Academic intellect isn't sufficient alone to become prosperous in life. IQ will be able to let you get work and make a full-time income; however, it cannot explain to you the way you can live a lifetime. In regards to success and joy in life, emotional wisdom makes it possible to build stronger connections, triumph in the office, and also reach your career and personal targets.

By improving the Emotional Intelligence (EI) of its employees, a firm may successfully influence two important trends identified in Patricia Aburdene's Megatrends 2010: "The Wave of Conscious Solutions" and "Spirituality in Business." Even as we enter this new age welcoming the widespread use of mindful methods in business, make sure your business is an earlier adopter, reaping the huge benefits on the competition who lag bogged by conventional small business beliefs. Emotional Intelligence, a mindful remedy to kneejerk reactionary emotional habits, could be your skill to acquire and apply knowledge in the emotions as well as the feelings of other people. The info regarding what you are feeling makes it possible to create effective decisions concerning what to say or perform (or not even say or perform).

It Allows You to utilize your emotions. That will assist you in making smarter decisions in-the-moment and possess significantly more effective control on you and your effect on the others. The idea of Emotional Intelligence is situated on brain research showing these skills are not the same as technical and cognitive abilities because they demand another portion of the brain - that the psychological center, the immune system, as opposed to the Neo Cortex. Emotional Intelligence is constituted of five primary principles. The initial step is knowing exactly what you are feeling. The 2nd reason is tackling your feelings, especially debilitating feelings. The 3rd is self-motivation, the fourth largest is compassion, and also the fifth is currently managing relationships.

Emotionally intelligent Men and Women can comprehend thEIr particular psychological condition and also the emotional states of the others, and consequently, they relate easily with people.

They hence communicate better, shape stronger connections, achieve increased success on the job, and lead a more fulfilling life. John Gottman was when he said "At the previous ten years or so, science has discovered that a significant amount regarding the role emotions plays in our lives. Researchers have discovered that more than IQyour emotional comprehension and abilities to take care of feelings can determine your success and enjoyment in most walks of life, including relationships."

Emotional Intelligence includes Five standard components, namely self-awareness, self-regulation, motivation, empathy and social capabilities. The very first three competencies are intra-personal and stress the way you can understand and manage yourself. Empathy and social skills are interpersonal competencies and stress your power to socialize and get on with other people. The greater your intra-personal abilities, the easier it becomes to extract your interpersonal skills. Mastering these skills will let you live a happier, happier and more successful and satisfying life.

Self-awareness is your very first component of emotional intelligence. It's the capacity to understand which emotions you're feeling and why. Whenever you know your emotions, then it's easier than you admit and restrain your feelings and stop your feelings out of judgment you. Additionally, you are convinced because you don't allow your emotions to escape control. Becoming self-explanatory also allows one to have a fair look at yourself and know your strengths and flaws, and also focus on those regions to accomplish superior outcomes for others and yourself.

Self-Regulation is your capability to Restrain your emotions and instincts and pick the emotions which you wish to experience in the place to be the prey of anything emotions arise. Whenever you can handle your emotional condition, it gets less difficult that you think before you act, which keeps you from making impulsive and poor conclusions. This ability also Enables You to transform adverse emotions that are exhausting to more positive and more effective types

The 3rd Part of psychological Intellect is motivation. That is about using your emotions to stay favorable, optimistic and consistent as opposed to pessimistic and negative. Whenever you get a high level of mental intelligence, you are inclined to be somewhat motivated, efficient and productive at what they are doing. Also, you make use of your feelings favorably to choose the proper action to persist and reach your goals even at the face of significant hardship or difficulty.

Empathy is the fourth largest component of Emotional brains. It's the capacity to genuinely comprehend and comprehend the emotions and standpoint of people across you. Empathetic individuals usually contain the power to listen effectively and directly into the others also are normally exceptional at managing relationships, improving communication, building confidence and about others.

The fifth Part of psychological Intellect is societal skills. Emotionally intelligent people today have great interpersonal skills and are great in maintaining and building relationships. Whenever you're exceptionally emotionally educated, you do not give attention to your success initially, and you also have other's desires at heart. You consistently promote an environment by which folks collaborate rather than contend together, and also you consistently help the others grow and develop.

Now psychological intelligence is a Secret to success in life, and also the fantastic thing is that regardless of your real amount of emotional intelligence, you also can improve it the perfect method to build up your mental abilities is through training. After that, you can are more effective at recognizing and handling your feelings in addition to the feelings of other people and lead a happier, more productive and satisfying life. Always bear in mind the wise words of Daniel Goleman that said, "What matters such as success, personality, happiness and prolonged accomplishments is a clear pair of psychological abilities - your EQ - perhaps not simply purely cognitive abilities which can be quantified by traditional IQ tests."

It's almost Sure That you've got Heard of the psychological quotient, EQ, along with psychological intelligence earlier, however, have you asked yourself if you're mentally intelligent? To go 1 step farther, are you currently mentally intelligent in the office? Think about BEIng a pioneer? When you've pondered those questions, then you might also have asked yourself why emotional intelligence is indeed vital. Within the following guide, I'll share more on the topic of emotional intelligence and its importance to every individual, every workplace, every society, and to even the complete world.

What's emotional intelligence?

Following psychologists Peter Salovey and John Mayer, emotional intelligence is "the ability to percEIve emotions, to access and generate emotions, to understand emotions and emotional knowledge, and to reflectively regulate emotions to promote emotional and cognitive growth" In lay man's terms, it's the degree to which we have been self-explanatory (able to comprehend and comprehend our emotions), may self-manage (in a position to accommodate and restrain our emotions and responses), may motivate ourselves (choosing the ideal action to attain an objective), could express compassion for different people, and also still have strong social skills (ability to develop positive connections with the others).

Emotional intelligence is quantified Through standardized evaluations, and the consequence of these evaluations is knas the Emotional Quotient (EQ). The greater the EQ will be, the better. But, unlike the Intelligence Quotient (IQ), that is usually adjusted by the time you reach a certain era, many scholars and scholars think that EQ is malleable and may be enriched and also heard.

Why is emotional intelligence Crucial?

EQ Might Not Be too renowned as IQ; however, many pros deem it important than IQ. Why? Studies reveal EQ is a much superior predictor of success, quality of connections, and enjoyment of somebody. It's clear anywhere and is crucial in every part of life. Maybe you have heard someone make announcements such as those: "Wow, what an optimistic person! He'll certainly reach something great in life" Or "She's very caring and social. She's such a fantastic boss" These comments attest that if an individual has high EQ (even though anyone doesn't understand it), it's felt and seen by the others. It's those forms of individual other tend to trust will probably attain accomplishment. Therefore, exactly why is EQ very important to everyone?

Inch. EQ is completely a significant Part of forming, developing, maintaining, and enhancing personal relationships with other individuals. It's indisputable that those who understand just how to develop positive connections with different men and women will almost certainly become prosperous within thEIr fields. Workers with higher EQ can operate invisibly in teams and conform to fluctuations. No matter how intelligent you're, in case you've got low emotional intelligence, you might come across the trail to success that a struggle. But there's excellent news. Enjoy knowing you may better your EQ skills at any age and regardless of past behavior.

2. Being Mindful of oneself Ways Becoming able to take care of constructive criticisms. You'd probably concur that there's not an ideal person on the planet and in what we do we want other people's criticisms and communicating to complete better. For those who get a high EQ, then you're self-indulgent, which means that you know your strengths, then admit your flaws, and also know exactly how your actions may affect different people

encircling you. Your high EQ enables you to shoot these criticisms bEIng the opportunity to advance your performance. This is an important section of working within an environment with several stakeholders.

3. Self-motivated Folks can Inspire everybody else. Each time a man or woman is self-motivated, the others around them regularly evaluate thEIr particular degree of motivation. A self-motivated man is optimistic and can be driven by exactly what things for him. Who wouldn't need a self-motivated man round, right? Motivation is infectious and also a highly-motivated household, workplace, or even society will outperform non-motivated kinds. Low-motivation might be an indication your emotional quotient is reduced in at least one of those crucial EQ quadrants.

4. EQ gets the entire world authentic. People who have a top Emotional Quotient have empathy which permits them to interact to the others within a "psychological level" If a man or woman can empathize with others, then afterwards she or he will get the job done genuinely and attend others' needs with empathy and maintenance; during times of struggle.

5. Using a top EQ means bEIng Able to restrain yourself in every situation. Your fellow worker yells in the angrily for an unknown motive. Given that this scenario, are you able to get a grip on your feelings rather than behave the same manner he did? You see, how EQ is attached to the way we restrain both our favorable and our destructive emotions. Think back again to some of those decisions on your lifetime you're not pleased with. Ask yourself just how a lot of them linked to a lack of self-control or too little impulse control? The solution might seem sudden.

Have you got higher clarity around What psychological intelligence and emotional quotient are? Do you concur it is more significant than bEIng "book-intelligent" or using a high IQ? Would you determine why EQ may be the trick to results? I reference mental intellect since the link. You know it if you find it, even if you can't spot it. The challenge is if emotional intelligence is overlooking, it's not always straightforward to spot. It's frequently obvious that a challenge exists but just what the issue is could be a puzzle.

Knowing what you understand concerning Mental intellect, I've got an issue for you. Ask yourself this question: Are you currently an emotionally intelligent person in your home and on the job? In case the solution is yes, then you're on the ideal path! Carry on along this course, strengthening your EQ skills while you proceed, and you might be well on the path to victory. If your response is no, don't stress. Emotional intelligence can be a group of skills you may improve with attention and also a solid plan. No matter where you stand now, you can't fail to purchase yourself and improving your emotional intelligence abilities.

Emotional Intelligence. This expression Keeps appearing anywhere at present; it had been mentioned about the Ryan Tubridy breakfast series today concerning big brother! What's crucial about Emotional Intelligence or E.I., and also exactly what value has this to you being an individual, on life, work and on your practice and development?

What decides Success?

Alfred Binet performed the earliest cognitive intellect evaluation from France in 1905. This later became famous as the Stanford Binet evaluation, and later it had been standardized at Stanford University for the population. Since that time, several have contended that test quantified one of their intelligence (the others incorporate emotional, spatial, musical, and artistic). But, it's taken more than 50 years to get Emotional Intelligence to be used seriously. Emotional Intelligence is the way we connect with ourselves, others and the environment generally. It's characterized by Dr Reuven baron, as any collection of non-cognitive skills, competencies, and skills that influence the ability to be successful in coping with environmental demands and anxieties; plus its one component in determining the capacity to flourish in lifespan.'

Most of us want to become Prosperous within our Resides and, until today, success equaled right As. The ordinary student frequently looked over the high achievers at school to be more lucrative than these were. Yet, the evidence doesn't prove to be the circumstance. Studies are completed after kids from school, through instant and forth into third level education. Then they came back in various stages to the very same individuals to test the way they were faring from the race referred to as lifetime, carrying in every aspect involving job, home and loved ones. What they found was that academic success doesn't necessarily equal 'being truly a victory'. The ordinary student was frequently very powerful when all elements of their lifetime were shot under an account, frequently obtaining the higher occupation and also more joyful homelife. Certainly, Cognitive Intelligence or even IQ is only one element in determining achievement, but there's still another intelligence in the drama, and that's Emotional Intelligence.

Unpredictable behavior

Have you worked in an environment where the air was stressed, as a result of the erratic behavior of a single penis? Would you remember (or are you currently experiencing) the worries that this kind of air causes? Have you noticed the domino effect that's on everybody at work? How will you work correctly in an environment similar to that if you're looking forward to a surprising outburst of uncontrolled anger, abuse, criticism or blame, abrupt highs or lows in the mood? This isn't just a healthy solution to work. Also, it's likewise not just a productive means to do the job. It's very stressful if this man or woman is a manager or manager.

People Today work better, and therefore are much more successful and effective if they're in a relaxed and happy environment. They'll require to go to work and also can continue to work more efficiently; they are also going to be inclined to add that excess work. Therefore how can you improve behavior, work air, and most of the associated places? The solution may be the use of Emotional Intelligence.

Using Emotional Intelligence

Daniel Goleman in his best-selling book, Emotional Intelligence: Why it can matter more than IQ (1995), defines E.I. because 'the capacity for recognizing our feelings and those of the others, for motivating ourselves for managing emotions well in ourselves and within our relationships.' The erratic member of this workforce clarified above failed to possess this capacity, so his coworkers suffered as an outcome. The capacity to handle feelings wasn't present, and also the abilities required to manage the pressures of normal living and work (as characterized by Dr Baron) weren't developed. His coworkers suffered on account of this dearth of emotional intelligence contained in this person. Emotional intelligence maybe with a lack of companies and teams generally. The fantastic news is that when aspects of weakness have been identified, at the person, company or team, they may be worked and improved.

There are many individuals associated With the developing understanding of E.I., one of them Peter Salovey and John Meyer, who at 1990 defined E.I. because 'the capability to track one's and others' feelings and emotions, to discriminate among them and to make use of this information to direct your thinking and activities.' This definition is quite pertinent to behavior within the task place also, if A-Workforce may act in this fashion, this might make an emotionally intelligent environment by the erratic behavior mentioned previously might not occur or might be handled efficiently if it didn't occur.

The Truth Is that no quantity of Development and training, team or education construction will possess authentic effect, even in case the E.I. of this average person or group is underdeveloped. The introduction and use of E.I. to corporate surroundings might fortify the good results of thEIr workforce generally speaking, regardless of what the size or activity of a business. E.I. is necessary in all levels and, even in case mature degrees adopt and employ E.I. into thEIr everyday dealings with peers and employees, this may filter through a business.

Be smart, Comply with the Footprints of intelligent folks, take their learnings and instruct them so you might grab the wisdom that they acquire. All these would be the stereotype statements created from our relatives, parents, senior and maybe even boss at the workplace.

This means being mindful and smart. In tackling the specific situation would be the trick to reevaluate the formulation of good results. What type of intellect are these guys speaking about? Are you currently speaking about logical intellect, including reasoning, discovering patterns, scientific analyses, de-coding creative and innovative thoughts, etc. Stress, anxiety, poor overall health, neglected relationship are the very best friends with the time that they also shed self-esteem and optimism in life.

Therefore, it's clear that logical Intelligence could push your success chart to a degree, however, saturate after some point. Is intellect truly the panacea for many of your anxieties and miseries. The answer would be yes, intellect socialized with feelings and emotions. It's knas mental intelligence.

What's emotional intelligence

Emotional intelligence is your ability to be conscious regarding the emotions, make and get into the feelings and handle our psychological prosperity to encourage our personal, spiritual and professional growth. The power is if you're completely privy to your feelings and restrain your activities and responses, and you're able to very quickly self-inspire and inspire everyone around, developing powerful connection and social skills together and express empathy for the others.

Twentieth-century exhibited the Chemical of IQ (Intelligence Quotient); people personality has been judged on the grounds of an intelligent quotient. In a onetime speech, the capacity to eventually become money-spinner and accord every luxury entity potential.

Various studies have indicated This it's a failed practice. To lead a happy, prosperous and productive lifetime emotional intelligence is demanded. Even though intelligent quotient is quantified under certain variables mental age and chronological period, however, psychological wisdom does not have any such parameters and will be enhanced at any given point of life.

Which are the advantages of EI

It's a false concept that psychological Intellect is just needed in the societal arena such as developing an excellent long-term relationship with the others; however, has a significant part of performing in each part of life. The Significant Advantages of emotional intelligence are:-

Stress-buster - Throughout our emotional intelligence certificate in Conducted each year, we put a huge focus on explaining the significance of emotional intelligence in releasing stress, stress and anxiety and achieving a superior condition of health.

Power to Deal with failure and Complaint absolutely - You will find not any praises and more gripe in life. An EI knows his strengths as well as the areas to use. He chooses criticism and failure another step closer to victory.

What's emotional intelligence and How do you benefit out of this? There is a significant range of definitions to get it. The majority of individuals will define this being an art where someone can synchronize his thoughts, and human body behaves through mind-control acts; a few specify the subject because of higher air instincts that aid a person answer situation. These people are right; some other person who is realized emotional cleverness creates tons of advantages within thEIr or her life. It's essential to comprehend a standard individual includes a particular level of mental intelligence; nevertheless, people may train thEIr heads to achieve high quantities with the art. You will find quite numerous informational websites that have step by step advice about what people can train thEIr minds to achieve psychological intelligence and these informational web sites are quite valuable to those who could be thinking about educating their heads to achieve psychological intelligence.

For anyone interested in accomplishing Mental intellect, afterwards developing the ideal mental attitude before engaging these behave determines of a person is likely to be more prosperous from the art. It's essential for an individual to develop view systems that are effectual beneficial in bringing the sort of success they would like to attain. An individual needs to also seek out advice about the way they can control or rather make the most of international legislation to influence the desired effect. Unlike what most believe, laws of appeal have become instrumental in forming a single personality. Individuals who encourage erroneous thoughts to audience thEIr heads more frequently not to need an extremely negative character which frees good overall life. It's essential to get somebody to coach thEIr heads to be optimistic in just about any particular situation since this can be the nature of not merely profiting emotional cleverness but also success in whatever that an individual does.

It Is Essential to Comprehend That attaining self-improvement acts in virtually any section of life isn't only a 1-day task. An individual needs to remain consistent and continuous in virtually any self-improvement action to attain the specified success. The degree for self-improvement success achievement will likely be quantified by campaigns someone is ready to put ahead towards attaining what she or he desires.

Individuals who have attained visuals of Mental brains have quite numerous benefits employed for them, for example, it's extremely feasible for people who've attained such success to Exude acts like telepathy, mind-reading and maybe even curing abilities. The ability of their heads. There's no limitation to that which an individual can achieve Through changing ability of their heads it's just necessary for anyone to generate an Interest and also a belief system they can perform the things that they want to realize Through electricity inside thEIr minds. As previously cited before viewing an excuse of What's emotional intelligence, folks could have different thoughts and Notions towards different meanings. But, accomplishing acts of psychological Intelligence are extremely advantageous to almost any individual interested in accomplishing almost any Lifetime success.

The three models

All these three chief types of mental intelligence carry a brand-new position inside the emotional attachment of people within their day to day activity and therefore forms the cornerstone. These generally include the capability model, the mixed version, and also the attribute model. We concentrate on David Goleman's mixed-model.

The six seconds style of emotional intelligence is just a procedure framework for obtaining and using feelings efficiently. Unlike other theoretical models, that is an incremental, practical, simple procedure which eases performance. The fundamental version, to the left, can be a cycle of three important pursuits.

The Four Aspects of Emotional Intelligence

You may have heard of mental intelligence, however also you might not know precisely what this means, therefore let us begin there. Essentially, emotional intelligence (EI) is all about recognizing and managing your emotions and many others. There's a solid research base in the fields of psychology, neuroscience, and small business leadership.

There are four basic facets of EI (as quantified by the emotional competence inventory, printed by the hay group): self-awareness, self-management, social awareness, and relationship management.

Self-awareness

This is how conscious you are and how correctly you can rate your emotions. The majority folks are so busy with the everyday grind we rarely have a step back and consider exactly how we're reacting to situations and the way we run into. The other supply of self-awareness is understanding how others answer us. That can be hard because we incline to find out which we would like to determine. And we are apt to prevent the uncomfortable act of asking the others for feedback.

To develop in yourself sense, look at building time for manifestation in every entire day. Also, think of stepping into the pattern of collecting special feedback from folks that are fair and also whose thoughts which you appreciate. A huge study that gathered tens of thousands of data found that pioneers that hunted out negative feedback proved far more self-reliant and effective than people that hunted out favorable feedback.

Self-management

Self-management is the skill to restrain your emotions. This component also has your transparency, adaptability, achievement, as well as confidence. A vital element is if you react or respond to both situations. Answer the questions:

If you obtain an irritating email, does one write straight away?

Can you sometimes end up regretting how you managed yourself, needing you had been calm and poised?

Can you shed rush or patience the others?

If you said yes to any of the questions, then you will be at the practice of responding in the place of reacting. Whenever you react, you can do what comes; naturally, that will be certainly going with all the emotional component of the human mind. Whenever you respond, you behave contrary to what's natural, that explains the reason why it's difficult. You participate in the logical portion of one's mind and pick out the ideal answer.

Social awareness

Your organizational consciousness, concentrate on support, and degree of compassion write your societal sense. Improve your organizational sense by finetuning your radar to the climate in classes, and realizing strength dynamics.

Enhance your ceremony orientation using your radar for the clients' or customers' needs. Try this by above all, always choosing personal responsibility when things are not going well. Other ways of boost your service orientation comprise bEIng available and receptive to your visitors as you can and thinking up something to collect feedback frequently.

Dating management

Developing others, functioning as a motivational leader and catalyst for change, cooperating using a self-study team, and managing conflict are part of relationship management.

You're high with this attribute in case the others percEIve you as likeable, and you are ready to utilize diverse classes, even at the face of tension and battle. Because you can see right now, to complete so necessitates the three faculties we've only discussed, and finesse in managing other individuals.

When you can create and convey an inspiring vision and assist them in completing things that are difficult, such as for instance, adopting shift, you're high with this particular characteristic.

How can you fare and exactly what will you farther grow to enhance your EI and livelihood operation?

The six seconds style of eq

The six moments version turns psychological intelligence concept into practice to the professional and personal life.

Emotional intelligence is the capacity to combine believing and sense to produce best decisions -- that will be essential to obtaining a fruitful relationship with others and yourself. To deliver a practical and easy solution to master and exercise mental intelligence, six moments developed a three-part version in 1997 as an activity -- an activity plan for implementing emotional wisdom in lifestyle.

This version of eq-in-action starts with three important interests: to are more aware (discovering what you can do), more deliberate (doing exactly what you intend), and much more meaningful (doing this for reasons).

Know your self

Seeing what you do and feel.

Emotions are statistics, and such competencies enable one to collect that info accurately.

Choose your self

Doing what you intend to do.

Rather than responding "on autopilot," these competencies permit you to respond proactively.

Give your self

Doing so for a motive.

These principles allow you to place your vision and mission to actions so that you lead purposely with complete ethics.

Know your self provides you precisely the "exactly what " -- whenever you understand yourself, you realize your challenges and strengths, do you understand what it is you do, everything you would like, and also what exactly things to improve.

Choose your self-supplies the "just how " -- it demonstrates how to do it, the way to influence others and yourself, how to "operationalize" those theories.

Give your self provides that the "why" --, whenever you give yourself-you, might be definite and active so that you keep focused just why to respond a certain way, the way to proceed around in brand new leadership, and others should return onboard.

You will see we present the version within a circle -- it is not a listing, but it's a procedure! This practice works whenever you twist it like a propeller moving a boat. As you proceed through those three pursuits, you attain favorable endings!

History of emotional intelligence

Even though through the history of intellect find out more about the attention was about the dimension of cognitive abilities, this process has also brought some criticism. One such longstanding criticism of this standard psychometric approach is that lots of theorists believe this tactic restricting and assert that, though IQ scores possess a particular validity and stability, they dismiss several other important facets of human operation

In this regard, since 1943, construction on the work of Thorndike, Wechsler started to discuss it non-cognitive facets of intellect: I've tried to demonstrate this furthermore to intellective.

Additionally, certain non-intellective facets influence intelligent behavior. In the event, these observations are correct; it seems that individuals can't expect to quantify total intelligence before our evaluations additionally incorporate some measures of these non-intellective facets.' (p. 103).

He afterwards described intelligence as the aggregate or international capacity of the person to act purposefully, to think logically, and also to cope effectively with his environment' (1958, 7). Robert Sternberg (1985) more recently suggested a 'triarchic' notion of intelligence, by which he contended that intellect is constituted of three individual factors; analytical, creative and practical. Sternberg's job is very important since it had been among those very first big concepts of intellect to comprise both cognitive and cognitive non-cognitive factors. It's also, hence, perhaps one of the very exhaustive concepts of intellect.

Sternberg's work helped to expand the scope of intellect, as he contended that IQ tests only measure certain facets of intellect and don't assess psychological and social things that influence everyday operation. As time passes, as theorists like Weschler and Sternberg started to question the effectiveness of this psychometric strategy and as an even substantial body of research has been performed in this respect, researchers began to realize that intellect had been not even close to an easy task to measure, and sometimes to even specify. By way of instance, Sternberg and Detterman, in 1987 asked 2 4 leading experts from the field to deliver a definition of this phrase 'intellect' and recEIved twenty-five unique definitions!

Thus, baron (1997) asserted it is more straightforward to quantify intelligence than it would be to specify it since researchers certainly encounter problems specifying intellect, but still prodigiously utilize intelligence testing in diverse settings. Additionally, several theorists have claimed that as opposed to simply being a unitary construct; intellect is certainly constituted of numerous different but linked constructs also that individuals ought to speak not to intellect in the impressive, however of multiple intelligences. By way of instance, Howard Gardner (1983) indicated that intellect is multi-faceted and contains both psychological and cognitive aspects. In his seminal text 'frames of mind, he asserted towards multiple intelligences and suggested there are EIght different kinds of individual intellect the following:

• linguistic intellect -- this field concerns verbal abilities, both written and spoken, for example, oration, studying, studying, writing and memory to dates and names.

A concise background of emotional intelligence

Peter Salovey and john d. Mayer coined the expression emotional intelligence' from 1990 describing it since "that a kind of social intelligence that involves the ability to track one's and others' feelings and emotions, to discriminate among them and to make use of this information to direct your thinking and activity".

Salovey and Mayer additionally initiated a research program meant to create valid measures of mental intelligence also to research its significance. For example, they found in 1 study when friends saw an upsetting picture, individuals that scored high emotional clarity (that will be the power to spot and then present a name into some mood which is being undergone) recovered quickly. In a second analysis, those who scored higher at the capacity to comprehend accurately, comprehend, and evaluate the others' emotions were able to react flexibly to changes within thEIr social surroundings and build supportive social support systems.

Daniel Goleman along with emotional intelligence

From the 1990s, Daniel Goleman became conscious of Salovey and Mayer's job, which finally resulted in his book, emotional intelligence. Goleman was a science fiction writer for the New

York Times, leading to brain and behavior research. He trained as a psychologist at Harvard where he worked together with David McClelland, and some others. McClelland was one of a growing band of investigators that have become worried about just how modest conventional tests of cognitive wisdom told us concerning what is necessary to be more prosperous in life.

Goleman contended it had been not cognitive wisdom which ensured business success, however emotional brains. He explained emotionally smart people as people using four traits:

they had been great at comprehending thEIr particular emotions (self-awareness)

they had been great at handling thEIr feelings (self-management)

they had been empathetic into the psychological drives of others (social consciousness)

they had been great at managing other people's emotions (social abilities)

The expression "psychological intelligence" seems first to have emerged at a 1964 paper by Michael Beldoch, also at the 1966 paper by b. Leuner qualified emotional wisdom and emancipation that seemed at the journal: the exercise of child psychology and child psychiatry.

Back in 1983, Howard Gardner's frames of mind: the theory of multiple intelligences introduced the concept that conventional kinds of intellect, for example, IQ, neglect to completely describe cognitive capability. He introduced the notion of multiple intelligences that comprised both social intelligence (that the capacity to know the goals, motives and motives of different people) along with intrapersonal intelligence (that the capability to comprehend oneself, to love the feelings, fears and motives).

The term then emerged in Wayne Payne's doctoral thesis, a report of emotion: developing emotional intelligence in 1985.

The earliest printed use of this word'eq' (emotional quotient) is an informative article by Keith Beasley at 1987 from the Mensa magazine.

In 1989 Stanley Greenspan submit a version to describe EI, accompanied closely by the following by Peter Salovey and John Mayer released from the subsequent calendar year.

Nevertheless, the expression became broadly called the book of Goleman's publication: psychological intelligence -- why it can matter more than IQ (1995). This would be for the publication's bestselling standing which the definition of could feature its popularity. Goleman has followed with a few further popular books of a very similar motif that fortify usage of the period. So far, tests quantifying EI never have substituted IQ tests bEIng a normal metric of intellect. Emotional intelligence has also recEIved criticism about its function in leadership and small business success. The differentiation between attribute mental intellect and skill mental brains premiered 2000.

Tips to increase emotional intelligence skills

Emotional intelligence, or eq, has been an ever more common skill to get from the world. Many could be wondering why emotional intelligence continues to rise in importance among peers at a growing workplace. In other words, mental intelligence isn't a fad. Significant businesses have compiled statistical proof that employees using emotional intelligence undoubtedly influence the main point. In reality, businesses with employees who have elevated degrees of emotional intellect see big gains in overall productivity and sales.

Emotional intelligence fuels your operation equally from the office, and on your life, however, it starts with you. From your confidence, compassion and confidence to your social abilities and self-control, handling and understanding your emotions may quicken victory in every area of one's life.

Regardless of what professional area you are in, whether you handle a group of 2 or 20, and maybe just yourself, denying how successful you're in controlling your very emotional energy can be an excellent starting place. Absent in the program, emotional intelligence isn't something we have been educated or analyzed on, so where did it originate out, exactly what can it be, are you experiencing it is it that important?

At an aggressive office, developing your eq skills is critical to your professional accomplishment. Below are ten ways to increase your eq:

1. Make use of an assertive design of communicating.

Assertive communication goes a long way toward earning admiration without sounding as overly aggressive or overly passive. Emotionally intelligent men and women understand just how to convey thEIr opinions and needs immediately while still respecting the others.

2. Respond rather than responding to battle.

Throughout cases of battle, psychological outbursts and feelings of anger are all common. The emotionally intelligent person knows just how to remain calm during stressful circumstances. They don't make spontaneous decisions which may cause even bigger issues. They know that in times of battle that the objective is a settlement, plus so they produce a conscious choice to concentrate on ensuring thEIr activities and words come in alignment with this.

3. Utilize active listening skills.

In discussions, emotionally smart people today listen to clarity as opposed to merely awaiting thEIr turn to speak. They make certain they know what's being said before reacting. Also, they focus on the non-verbal specifics of a dialogue. This prevents mistakes, enables the consumer to respond precisely and shows admiration to your person they have been talking with.

4. Be moved.

Emotionally intelligent men and women are thEIr attitudes to motivate others. They establish goals and therefore are resilient facing challenges.

5. Practice approaches to keep a favorable attitude.

Do not underestimate the energy of one's attitude. An unfavorable attitude readily amazes the others when an individual lets it. Emotionally intelligent folks possess an understanding of the moods of those around them and protect their attitude consequently. They are aware of what they will need to complete to be able to have a fantastic day and a positive prognosis truly. This might include using a terrific lunch or breakfast, doing meditation or prayer throughout your daytime or storing positive quotes in thEIr computer or desk.

6. Exercise self-awareness.

Emotionally intelligent men and women are self-explanatory and instinctive. They have been conscious of their feelings and the way they can influence those around them. Additionally, they pick up on the others' emotions and body language and utilize that advice to better thEIr communication abilities.

7. Take review well.

A vitally significant part increasing your psychological intelligence would be to accept review. Rather than becoming confused or high eq people take a couple of minutes to comprehend at which the review is originating from, how it's affecting their operation and the way they're able to resolve any difficulties constructively.

8. Empathize with other people.

Emotionally intelligent men and women understand the best way to empathize. They know that compassion is a feature which shows emotional strength, not weakness. Empathy helps you to connect with the others onto a simple human grade. It unlocks the doorway for mutual respect and understanding between people with diverse opinions as well as situations.

9. Utilize leadership abilities.

Emotionally intelligent individuals have exceptional leadership abilities. They will have high standards for themselves and set a good example for the others to observe. They take the initiative and possess great decision problem-solving and making skills. This allows getting a much higher and more efficient degree of operation in life and on the job.

10. Be approachable and social.

Emotionally intelligent men and women come off approachable. They grin and give a confident presence. They work with appropriate social skills dependent on thEIr partnership with whomever they're around. They will have great social skills and understand just how to convey clearly; perhaps the communication is nonverbal or verbal.

A number of these abilities may appear to be greatest suited for people that know human psychology. While high eq skills can come more readily to naturally empathetic folks, everyone could form them. Less empathetic individuals merely need to practice bEIng self-aware and alert to the way they socialize with other individuals. By applying these measures, you will be well on the road to a growth in your mental intelligence degree.

These eight hints farther supply a fantastic beginning point to finding the foundations of one's mental intelligence.

1) exercise celebrating how you are feeling

Frequently we guide hectic, busy lifestyles plus it are all too possible for people to shed contact your emotions. To reconnect, consider setting a timer for a variety of points throughout your afternoon. After the timer goes away, have several deep breaths and then notice the way, you are feeling mental. Look closely at where that emotion is currently turning as a physical sense on the human body, and the impression seems just like. The longer you exercise, the longer it'll become 2nd nature.

2) focus on how you act

During the time you are practicing your psychological consciousness, take time to notice that your behavior too. Detect how you behave if you are experiencing certain feelings, and also how that affects your daily life. Managing our feelings becomes simpler as we are conscious of how we answer them.

3) ask your personal opinions

Within this hyper-connected globe, it isn't difficult to fall in and comment bubble'. This is a condition of presence where your remarks are continuously reinforced by people who have similar perspectives. Make care to browse the flip side of this narrative and also have your views challenged (even when you still believe that they have been right). This can allow you to know different people and start to become receptive to fresh thoughts.

4) take responsibility for the emotions

Your emotions and behavior originate from you; they don't result from anybody else and once you get started accepting responsibility for the way you're feeling and the way you act it may have a good effect on every area of one's life.

5) take the time to observe the favorable

A vital part of psychological intellect is observing and reflecting on the optimistic moments in everyday life. Individuals who undergo positive emotions are normally more resilient and much more inclined to have fulfilling relationships that'll assist them in proceeding forward away from hardship.

6) but do not discount the unwanted

Reflecting on negative emotions is equally as important as representing the favorable. Recognizing why you're feeling drawback is essential to learning to be a fully rounded individual, that can manage negative problems later on.

7) do not forget to breathe

Life throws different scenarios in our manner, with the majority folks undergoing some form of stress on a normal basis. To handle your emotions at these times also to steer clear of outbursts, do not forget to breathe. Call out a time and move put some cold water onto your head and go outdoors and get some outdoors or earn a beverage -- whatever to maintain your cool and provide an opportunity to obtain a grip on what's happening and how you need to respond.

8) a life procedure

Know and bear in mind that emotional intelligence is something which you grow and necessitates continual advancement; it's greatly a life practice.

Self-awareness

A vital part of emotional intelligence, self-awareness could be your capacity to determine and comprehend your character, feelings and moods and thEIr effect on the others. It has a realistic self-assessment about that which you are capable of --

your strengths and flaws -- and focusing on exactly how others perceived you. It helps highlight areas for self-indulgent, which makes you better in adapting and certainly will limit wrong decisions.

9) learn how to check at yourself

Knowing your self is difficult and it's nearly impossible to check at yourself, therefore enter from people that understand you're crucial. Ask them where your weaknesses and strengths lie, jot exactly what they say and also compare it. Keep an eye out to almost any designs and recall to not contend together with it -- they are only hoping to allow you to judge your perception out of the other's viewpoint.

10) maintain a journal

A fantastic solution to find a precise estimate of your self would always be to keep a journal. Start by writing exactly what happened for you at the close of every single day, just how it made you feel and the way you coped with it. Documenting details such as these is likely to leave you aware of what you are doing and also certainly will highlight where issues may be coming out of. Gradually, return over your comments and also pay attention to some trends.

11) understand what inspires you

Everybody else includes a core motivation whenever they begin a job. The issue is keeping this driving force at heart when hardship appears. Frequently people begin a job but don't accomplish it as they lose thEIr motivation to achieve that. Make care to comprehend what inspires you personally and use it to push one across the end.

12) have it simple

Sometimes emotional outbreaks happen because we do not take out time to slow and process just how we're feeling. Give yourself some slack and create a careful attempt to meditate, do yoga or see -- tiny escapism works wonders. After which next time, you might have a psychological reaction to a person, make an effort to pause until you react.

13) acknowledge your psychological triggers

Self-aware people can reevaluate their emotions because they occur. It's critical to be flexible with your feelings and also adapt them to your situation. Do not deny your emotions period time but tend not to be stiff using them; take some opportunity to process your feelings prior to conveying them.

14) predict the way you'll sense

Look at a scenario you are going to and predict the way you may feel. Practice pruning and accepting the feelings - assessing the atmosphere sets you in control. Make an effort to opt for a proper reaction to the atmosphere as opposed to simply responding to it.

15) trust your instinct

If you remain unsure about which course to choose, trust your instinct. Your subconscious was learning that course to take all through your whole life.

16) snap out of it

One key means to maintain your emotions in balance is to modify your sensory input signal -- motion dictates emotion while the old expression goes. So jolt your body outside of regular by attending a fitness class or take to channeling a crowded mind using a mystery or even a publication - whatever to violate your current routine.

17) keep a program (and stay with it!))

Ensuring you produce a program and stick with it is vitally crucial when you would like to accomplish tasks effortlessly.

If you schedule appointments on your calendar, then you are saying to yourself "I am going to do a, c and b date and it's going to require y hours. "Once you create this particular claim, it gets tougher to procrastinate."

Why Developing Emotional Intelligence Is Important
What's the need for emotional intelligence?

The term 'psychological intelligence', first coined by psychologists Mayer and Salovey (1990), identifies the capacity to comprehend the procedure and modulate emotional advice accurately and effortlessly, both within oneself and others and also to make use of this information to direct your thinking and activities also to influence people others.

Mental intelligence can direct us on the trail to a satisfied and joyful life by providing a frame whereby to employ standards of intellect into emotional answers and comprehend that these answers could be consistent or inconsistent with special beliefs regarding emotion.

While the workplace evolves, so too can your human body of research encouraging that individuals (out of interns to managers) with higher EI are better designed to work independently within teams, handle change effectively, and manage stress -- thereby permitting them to pursue business objectives efficiently.

Goleman (1995) established five different sorts of skills that form the critical qualities of EI and suggested that, unlike the intelligence quotient (IQ), those categorical skills are learned at which sprinkled and superior where present.

So, EI, despite its relatively predetermined cousin, IQ, is alternatively a lively facet of someone's mind and comprises behavioral characteristics which, when worked, can yield substantial advantages, from personal happiness and wellbEIng to raised success at a specialist context.

Worth and benefits of emotional intelligence

The significance and advantages of mental intelligence are immense concerning professional and personal success. It's just a core competency in most vocations, can encourage the progress towards professional and academic success, improve relationships, and enhance communicating abilities, and the list continues.

It is worthy of note to go up to now suggesting that people who have higher EI tend to do better compared to people who have lesser EI in lifetime complete, aside from IQ. There's been much debate concerning the great things about teaching EI in schools, having a focus on the thought that emotionally intelligent kids mature to become mentally educated adults.

Proficiency in EI is turning into an essential requirement in protracted or intense regions of 'emotional work' such as nursing, and social work, both the service business and management functions. High EI boosts the physical and psychological health of the people and promotes academic and small business performance.

Mental intellect is an essential component of developing and forming purposeful human connections. It is discovered, over a collection of studies, there have been significant connections between top EI and much more powerful social connections. Those participants that exhibited elevated degrees of EI also revealed a larger propensity for empathic view shooting, collaboration with the others, developing caring and much more fulfilling connections in addition to more social skills generally.

Thus much, we've dedicated to the societal and psychological advantages of both EI; it's necessary to be aware the self-awareness -- that the ability to handle stress and emotions -- and also the capacity to fix personal, in addition to societal troubles, may also be somewhat linked to physical wellbEIng.

Chronic stress and the protracted unwanted effects that accompany it as anger, depression, and stress may induce the onset and development of hypertension, obesity, heart problems, and diabetes; growth susceptibility to viruses, viruses, and ailments; delay curing of injuries and wounds; and also aggravate conditions such as atherosclerosis and arthritis.

The significance of EI is immense; growing psychological intelligence promotes many positive traits, ranging from endurance to communicating, motivation to worry control, most which can be viewed as conducive to effortlessly achieving physical, personal and occupational health, and success.

We tend to think of our feelings and our intellect as just two different things. But put them together as emotional intelligence, and it is an alternative method to become smart as it has "that the capacity to know about control, and express the emotions, and also to manage social relationships judiciously and empathetically" in line with this dictionary definition.

· **self-awareness:** whenever we're self-indulgent, we understand our strengths and flaws, in addition to the way we respond to people and situations.

• **self-regulation:** since they truly are self-explanatory, emotionally intelligent men and women may control thEIr feelings and maintain them as vital.

• **motivation:** individuals with high emotional intelligence tend to be exceptionally motivated, also, making them resilient and optimistic.

• **empathy:** individuals with compassion and empathy are simply just better at linking with other men and women.

• **social skills:** the social skills of mentally intelligent men and women reveal they care for and respect the others, and so they get along well together.

Exactly why EQ is needed at work

Just as you walk throughout the doorway and into an office building doesn't indicate that you assess your emotions in the doorway before beginning, even though it used to appear like that. Emotions happen to be at the workplace; however, these must be retained in balance, together with people pretending never to feel while these were about the clock.

Nowadays, however, we're allowing emotions on the job and recognizing the advantages of doing this. And emotional intelligence matters a lot more than it used to as the workplace has shifted. Now we work chiefly in teams, not isolation, so for starters, and informed organizations realize that understanding emotions exist could cause wholesome surroundings. It won't indicate it's a psychological free-for-all by anyway; however, it can mean people are much more likely to know about the owner and others' emotions and behave so. People who have high emotional intelligence are somewhat more elastic to improve a must within our fast-changing electronic age.

Additionally, leaders, together with higher psychological brains, generally have happier employees who subsequently stay more, reducing the expenses of attrition, and also strive harder rising productivity. An informative article at Forbes cites samples of salespeople with higher mental intelligence somewhat outperforming additional salespeople," also says in the research of 5 15 executives, mental intellect was a greater predictor of succeeding compared to just experience or IQ.

Businesses which are hiring want to be certain they choose job applicants that will mesh well with existing teams. Because of this, roughly 20 per cent of associations are currently analyzing for emotional intelligence included in thEIr marketing procedures. The cleverest man needs good people skills to achieve success nowadays. A top IQ alone is no more.

The Way to Enhance Your Emotional Intelligence

A higher IQ can be something we tend to get born while psychological wisdom is something we could work to improve. Into a large extent, our mental intelligence starts in youth with exactly how we're raised, but as adults, we may take action to get mentally "brighter" Justin barista, writer of eq," applied: a real-world method of emotional intelligence, provides seven methods to enhance emotional intelligence within a post written for inc:

· **reflect in your emotions.** This is the area where self-awareness begins. To increase emotional intelligence, think in your emotions and how you typically respond to adverse scenarios, whether or not they call for some co-worker, relative or even stranger. Whenever you are more conscious of one's emotions and typical reactions, then you may begin to regulate them.

· **request perspective.** That which we perceived to be the truth is frequently quite distinct from what people around us are visiting. Start getting input from other people to comprehend the way you encounter in emotionally charged cases.

• **observe.** When you have increased your self-awareness, and you also comprehend the way you are coming up, pay more attention to your emotions.

• **wait for a minute.** Stop and think before you speak or act. It's difficult to perform, however, keep working on it and it's going to become an addiction eventually.

• **become more impressed by knowing the "why."** attempt to comprehend that the "why" behind the other individual's emotions or feelings.

• **elect to study on criticism**. Who enjoys criticism? Maybe nobody. Nonetheless, it's inevitable. As soon as we elect to study from criticism instead of only shield our behaviors, we could grow in emotional brains.

• practice, practice, practice. Becoming emotionally apt won't happen immediately; however it sometimes happens --together with patience, effort, and a great deal of practice.

We live in an era when we may make a certificate in just about any range of themes to boost our careers, as a result of technology, but we cannot bring in one in mental intelligence. That is something we must tackle as humans, to comprehend it as significant, opt to improve it continue working about it probably for the remainder of our lives. However, the payoffs are worthwhile as we become much better employees, better partners, and all-around better people.

CHAPTER TWO
HOW TO MANAGE ANGER

Recognizing anger

Faith is a normal, wholesome emotion, nEIther very good nor bad. Like every emotion, it communicates a note, telling you a circumstance is troubling, unjust, or threatening. If your knee jerk reaction to anger is always to burst, but that message does not get an opportunity to be hauled. Therefore, while it's absolutely normal to feel mad once you've been abused or wronged, anger gets to be a real challenge once you say it in a manner that hurts others or yourself.

You may believe that venting your anger is healthy, which the people around you're overly sensitive, so your anger is warranted, or you will need to show your fury to find esteem. However, the reality is that anger is a whole lot more inclined to possess a negative influence on how people visit you personally, impair your decision, and also enter the method of succeeding.

Effect of Anger

Chronic anger which illuminates all of the time upward or pops out of control could have serious impacts on the: physical wellness. Consistently operating at elevated degrees of both stress and anger leaves you more vulnerable to cardiovascular problems, diabetes, a weakened immune system, insomnia, and higher blood pressure.

Emotional wellbeing. Chronic anger absorbs a large amount of energy, your thinking, which makes it tougher to concentrate or love lifetime. Also, it can result in depression, stress, and other emotional health difficulties.

Career. Constructive criticism, creative gaps, and heated argument can be healthier. But lashing out alienates your coworkers, managers, or customers and erodes their esteem relationships. Anger can induce lasting scars from the people that you like most and acquire in the way of friendships and work relationships. Explosive anger causes it almost impossible for other people to trust one, speak frankly, or come to feel comfortable and can be particularly damaging for kids.

In case you have a hot temper, then you will feel as if it's from the hands and there is little you can do to tame the monster. However, you need more control over your anger than you believe. With comprehension about the genuine causes of the anger and also all these anger control applications, you may learn how to express your feelings without even damaging the others and maintain your mood from mimicking your life.

The objective of anger management is to reduce your emotional feelings and the physiological arousal that anger causes. You cannot be rid, or even avoid, the things or the people who enrage you, nor will you change them, but you may learn how to control your responses.

Are you angry?

There are psychological evaluations that assess the intensity of angry feelings, how prone to anger you're, and also how you handle it. However, the odds are good that if you have an issue with anger, then you know it. If you end up behaving in ways which seem out of control and frightening, you may want help finding better methods to address this particular emotion.

Are some people angrier than others?

Some folks are somewhat more "hotheaded" than others are they become angry more easily and more intensely than the normal man does. Additionally, some people do not reveal their anger in loud spectacular ways but are chronically irritable and grumpy. Easily angered people do not always curse and throw things; sometimes, they withdraw socially, sulk, or becoming physically ill.

Individuals that are easily angered generally have what some psychologists call a low tolerance for frustration, meaning that they believe they need not need to be exposed to frustration, inconvenience, or annoyance. They cannot simply take things in stride, and they're particularly infuriated if the situation seems somehow unjust: for instance, is corrected for a minor mistake.

What makes these people in this way? Several items. One cause may be genetic or bodily: there's evidence that some children are born irritable, touchy, and easily angered, and that these signs are present from the young age. Yet another could be sociocultural. Anxiety can be considered negative; we're taught it is fine to express anxiety, depression, or other emotions but not to express anger. Because of this, we do not know the way to handle it or channel it constructively.

Research has also discovered that household background plays an important job. On average, individuals who are easily angered come from families that are disruptive, disorderly, and not skilled at emotional communications.

Might it be good to "let it all hang out?"

Psychologists now say that it is a dangerous fantasy. Many folks use this theory for a license to hurt the others. Studies have discovered that "letting it rip" with anger escalates anger and aggression and does nothing whatsoever to aid you (or anyone who you're angry with) resolve the circumstance.

It is ideal for learning what it's that activates your anger and to develop strategies to keep those triggers from tipping you over the border.

Comfort

Simple relaxation tools, such as heavy breathing and relaxing imagery, can help calm angry feelings. You will find books and courses that will teach you relaxation methods, and after you learn the methods, you're able to call upon them at virtually any circumstance. If you take part in a relationship where both spouses are hot-tempered, then it may be a fantastic idea for the two of you to master those methods.

Some easy measures you can attempt:

· breathe deeply, from your diaphragm; breathing from your chest will not relax you. Picture your breath coming up from your "gut."

· slowly repeat a calm word or phrase such as "relax," go easy." repeat it to yourself while breathing deeply.

· use vision; envision a relaxing experience, from EIther your memory or your imagination.

· non-strenuous, slow yoga-like exercises can relax your muscles and allow you to feel much healthier.

Follow these techniques daily. Learn to utilize them automatically whenever you are in a stressed situation.

COGNITIVE RESTRUCTURING

In other words, this implies altering the way you believe. Angry people tend to curse, swear, or speak in highly colorful terms that reflect thEIr inner mind. Whenever you are angry, your thinking can get very exaggerated and overly dramatic. Consider replacing these thoughts with more rational types. For example, rather than telling yourself, "oh, it's horrible, it's terrible, everything's ruined," tell yourself, "it's frustrating, and it's clear that I am mad about this; however, it isn't exactly the ending of the planet and getting angry isn't going to fix it anyway."

Remind yourself that getting angry is maybe not going to deal with anything, it won't cause you to feel a lot better (and may make you feel worse).

Logic defeats anger, because anger, anger even if it is justified, can quickly become irrational. So use cold hard logic on yourself. Inform yourself that the planet is "not to get you," you are just experiencing some of those rough spots of everyday life. Try that whenever you feel anger getting the best of you, plus it is going to let you get a more balanced outlook. Angry people tend to demand things: fairness, appreciation, agreement, willingness to do things in thEIr way. Everybody needs these things, and we're all hurt and disappointed if we do not buy them, but angry men and women demand them when thEIr requirements are not met, thEIr disappointment becomes anger. Included in these cognitive restructuring, angry men and women will need to become aware of the demanding nature and translate thEIr expectations into desires.

To put it differently, saying, "I'd like" something is healthier than just saying, "I demand" or "I must have" something. Whenever you are not able to get exactly what you would like, you are going to go through the normal responses --frustration, frustration, hurt--however, maybe anger. Some angry men and women use this anger as a means to prevent feeling hurt, but this does not mean the hurt goes off.

Problem-solving

Sometimes, our anger and frustration are triggered by very real and inescapable problems in our lives. Not all anger is misplaced, and usually, it is a healthy, natural response to such difficulties. There's also a cultural belief that every problem has an answer, plus it adds to the frustration to see that isn't always the situation. The best attitude to bring to such a circumstance, then, would be not to concentrate on finding the solution, but instead how you handle and face the dilemma.

Produce a plan, and assess out your advancement over the way. Resolve to give it the absolute best, but also not to punish yourself if an answer does not come straight away. If you can approach it with your best intentions and efforts and make a serious effort to handle it, you will not be as inclined to shed patience and fall to re believing, even when the situation doesn't get solved straight away.

Better Communication

Angry people often jump to--and also behave on--decisions, and several of these decisions can be quite inaccurate. The first action to take in case you are in a heated discussion is slow and consider your answers. Do not state the first issue comes to your mind, but slow and think carefully about everything you would like to state. At precisely the same time, listen attentively to what another person says and take your time before replying.

Listen, also, to what's underlying the anger. As an example, you enjoy some freedom and individual space, as well as your "significant other", wants more connection and closeness. When she or he starts complaining about your activities, do not retaliate by painting your partner as a jailer, a warden, or an albatross around your neck.

It is natural to get defensive if you're criticized, but do not fight. Alternatively, tune in to what's underlying the words: the message this individual may feel neglected and unloved. It might take a great deal of patient questioning on your area; also it might need some breathing space, however, do not allow your anger--or even perhaps a partner's, let a discussion spin out of control. Keeping your cool can keep the situation from becoming a disastrous one.

Utilizing humor

"Silly humor" can help defuse rage in many of means. For starters, it will be able to let you get a more balanced outlook. Whenever you become angry and call someone a name or consult with them in some imaginative phrase, stop and picture what that word would look like. If you are in the office and you also consider a co-worker as a "dirtbag" or perhaps a "single-cell lifestyle," as an instance, picture a big bag filled with dirt (or an amoeba) sitting in your colleague's desk, talking on the telephone, visiting meetings. Do this whenever a name comes into your head about someone else. If you can draw a picture about just what the real thing might look like. This is going to need a great deal of the edge of your fury, and humor can always be depended upon to help unknot a tense state of affairs.

The underlying message of highly angry people, dr. Deffenbacher says, is "things ought to go my way" angry people often believe they are morally right, that any blocking or changing of thEIr plans is an unbearable indignity and that they should perhaps not have to undergo in this way. Maybe other folks do, however, not them!

If you feel that urge, he proposes, envisions yourself like a god or goddess, a supreme ruler, that possesses the roads and stores and office space, striding alone and having your way in all situations while others defer to you personally. The more detail you can go into your imaginary scenes, the more opportunities you need to appreciate that perhaps you might be bEIng foolish; you will also realize how unimportant the things you are angry about are. There are two cautions in using humor. To begin with, do not make an effort to "laugh off" your issues; rather, use humor to help yourself face them more constructively. Secondly, do not cave into harsh, sarcastic humor; that is only another kind of unhealthy anger expression.

These methods have in common is a refusal to take yourself too badly. Anger is a serious emotion, but it's usually accompanied by ideas that, if examined, can make you laugh.

Shifting your environment

Sometimes it's our immediate surroundings which give us cause for irritation and fury. Problems and responsibilities can weigh on you and cause you to feel mad at the "snare" you seem to have fallen into and all of the people and things that form that trap.

Give yourself some slack down. Be sure to have some "personal time" scheduled for times of this day you know are particularly vulnerable. One of these is the working mother with a standing rule that after she's back home from work, for its initial fifteen minutes "nobody talks to Mom unless the house is unstoppable " after this brief quiet time, she feels better prepared to handle demands from her kids without blowing them up.

Various other strategies for easing on your self

Period: if you and your partner are inclined to fight when you discuss things at night--perhaps you are tired, or angry, or perhaps it's simply dependency --try changing the occasions when you speak about important matters, so these talks do not become debates.

Avoidance: if your child's chaotic space makes you furious every time you walk through it, close your door. Do not create yourself look at what infuriates you. Remember, "well, my child should clean the room up so that I won't need to be mad!" that is not exactly the purpose. The point would be to remain calm.

Finding alternatives: if your everyday walk through traffic leaves you into a situation of anger and frustration, and give a job --learn or map out another path, the one that is less curable or maybe more scenic. Or find another alternative, such as a bus or commuter train.

Ten tips to increase your anger management

But, anger can get problematic in case it contributes to aggression, outbursts, and sometimes physical altercations.

Anger controller is essential for assisting you to avoid doing or saying something that you will regret. Before anger escalates, you should use certain strategies for controlling anger.

Below are ways you can restrain your anger: · count down

Count d(or up) into 10. If you are extremely angry, start at 100. At the time that it takes one to count, and your heartbeat will slow down, and your anger will probably subside.

· require a breather

Your breathing becomes shallower and rates up while you get mad. Reverse this tendency (along with also your anger) by simply taking slow, deep breaths in the nose and exhaling from your mouth for several minutes.

· go stroll round

Calm your nerves and decrease anger. Opt for a walk, ride your bike, or hit a few golf balls. Whatever which gets your limbs draining is great for the body and mind.

· duplicate a headline

Locate a word or word that can help you settle and refocus. Repeat this word again and to yourself, once you are angry. "relax," go easy, and "you will be okay" are good examples.

· stretch

Neck rolls and shoulder rolls are all good samples of non-strenuous yoga-like moves which could enable you to restrain the entire body and exploit your emotions. No fancy equipment demanded.

· mentally escape

Slip to a quiet space, close your mind, and clinic picturing yourself at a relaxing spectacle. Give attention to details from the fanciful landscape: what color is your water? Just how tall are the hills? Exactly what would the chirping birds seem like? This clinic is able to assist you in finding calm amidst anger.

· play any songs

Let audio take away you from your feelings. Devote ear-buds or slide out to your vehicle. Crank up your favorite music (avoid heavy metal and rock), and hum, bop, or sashay your anger off.

· stop talking

When you're steamed, so you may well be tempted to allow mad words fly; however, you are more inclined to do harm than good. Pretend your lips have been glued closed as you did as a young child. This moment without speaking can provide you the time to get your thoughts.

· require a time out

Give a rest. Sit far from your others. Within this silent period, you're able to process events and reunite your emotions to impartial. You are even allowed to locate away this time from the others is so helpful you desire to program it in your everyday routine.

· do it

Harness your energy. Subscribe to a request. Write an email to an official. Do something great for somebody else. Expand your time and emotions into something productive and healthy.

The most important thing

Anger is a standard emotion that everyone experiences from time to time. But if you locate your anger turns out to aggression or outbursts, then you want to get healthier ways to manage anger.

If these tips do not help, think about talking with your health care provider. A mental health therapist or therapist will be able to assist you to function with inherent factors which could bring about anger and other mental troubles.

Emotional disorder

Emotional illness also referred to as psychological health ailments, describes to a vast assortment of mental health issues -- ailments which change your mood, thinking and behavior. Cases of an emotional disease involve depression, anxiety disorders, schizophrenia, and eating disorders and addictive behaviors.

Many men and women think that psychological ailments are infrequent and "occur to another person." in reality, emotional disorders are widespread and common. Around 54 million Americans suffer from some emotional illness in a particular calendar year.

Most households aren't prepared to deal with studying thEIr loved person has a mental disease. It might be emotionally and physically stressful, and could make us feel at risk of the opinions and conclusions of the others.

If you believe that you or someone you know might have a psychological or psychological problem, it's crucial to consider that there were help and hope.

Most men and women have emotional health issues every once in a while. However, a psychological health problem gets to be a mental disease when ongoing indications cause frequent stress and affect your capability to operate.

A psychological disease may make you unhappy and will cause issues in your ordinary life, like in the work or school in relationships. Typically, symptoms may be handled with a variety of medications and talk therapy (psychotherapy).

Infection

Evidence and indicators of the mental disease may fluctuate, based upon the disease, circumstances and different aspects. Emotional disorder symptoms may affect emotions, thoughts and behaviors.

Cases of symptoms and signs involve:

· feeling for miserable

· confused believing or decreased capacity to focus

· extortionate anxieties or anxieties, or intense feelings of remorse

· extreme mood effects of highs and lows

· withdrawal from friends and actions

· significant fatigue, low electricity or issues sleeping

· detachment from reality (delusions), paranoia or hallucinations

· inability to cope with everyday issues or anxiety

· trouble understanding and about scenarios and also to individuals

· issues with alcohol or medication use

· significant changes in eating customs

· sex drive varies

· intense anger, hostility or violence

· suicidal thinking

Sometimes indicators of a mental health disease appear as physical issues, such as abdominal pain back pain, headache, or some other unexplained pains and pains.

Reasons

Emotional illnesses, generally speaking, are believed to result from an assortment of environmental and genetic facets:

· inherited attributes. Mental disease is more prevalent in people whose blood family members also have an emotional disease.

Certain genes might raise your chance of creating a mental disease, and also your life situation can activate it.

· environmental exposures before arrival. Contact with environmental ailments, inflammatory diseases, alcohol, toxins or drugs during the uterus can occasionally be associated with the emotional disease.

· brain chemistry. Neurotransmitters are naturally occurring brain chemicals that carry signals to various pieces of one's body and brain. If the neural tissues between these compounds are diminished, the purpose of neural receptors and neural technIQues vary, resulting in depression and other psychological ailments.

Risk variables

Certain facets might increase your chance of creating a mental disease, for example:

· a report on psychological illness at a blood relative, like a sibling or parent

· stressful life scenarios, for example, fiscal issues, a family member's departure or even a divorce

· a continuing (chronic) health illness, like diabetes

· brain harm due to a serious injury (traumatic brain injury), like a vicious blow to the mind

· traumatic adventures, such as military battle or attack

· the use of alcohol or psychiatric drugs

· a childhood history of neglect or abuse

· a few buddies or couple of healthful connections

· a prior mental disease

The emotional disease is not uncommon. Approximately 1 in 5 adults has a mental illness in any particular calendar year. The emotional disease can begin at any age, from childhood through after mature years; however, many cases begin sooner in life.

The consequences of mental disorder might be temporary or long-lasting. Additionally, you could have more than a mental health disease at precisely the same moment. As an instance, you might have depression and a substance use disorder.

You will find more than 200 classified forms of psychological disease. A number of the common disorders are depression, bipolar illness, dementia, schizophrenia and stress disorders.

Symptoms could include changes in mood, personality, personal habits or societal lack of

Emotional health issues could be related to excess stress because of a certain circumstance or sequence of events. Much like cancer, obesity, diabetes and cardiovascular problems, mental disorders are usually physical in addition to emotional and emotional. Mental illnesses could result from a reaction to environmental stresses, genetic factors, biochemical imbalances, or a mixture of them. With appropriate treatment and care, a lot of people learn how to cope or recover from an emotional disease or psychological illness.

Infection

Emotional illness is a primary cause of handicap. Untreated mental illness could result in severe emotional, behavioral and emotional health issues. Complications occasionally associated with emotional disease contain:

· unhappiness and diminished pleasure of existence

· family conflicts

· dating problems

· social isolation

· issues with alcohol, tobacco and other medications

83

· missed school or work, or other issues associated with school or work

· legal and fiscal issues

· poverty and homelessness

· self-harm and injury to other people, such as suicide or homicide

· weakened immune system, so that your body has trouble resisting diseases

· heart disease and other health ailments

Many typical kinds of

· clinical melancholy

A mental health disease characterized by consistently depressed mood or lack of interest in action, resulting in substantial impairment in lifestyle.

· stress disease

A mental health illness evidenced with feelings of stress, anxiety or anxiety, which are strong enough to restrict one's activities.

· bipolar disease

A disease-related to episodes of mood swings which range from manic highs to manic highs.

· **dementia**

Several believing along with societal symptoms which interferes with daily operation.

· **attention-deficit/hyperactivity disorder**

A chronic condition, for example, attention problem, hyperactivity and impulsiveness.

· **schizophrenia**

A disease that affects a person's power to think, feel and act naturally.

· **obsessive-compulsive disorder**

Extortionate ideas (obsessions) that contribute to persistent behaviors (compulsions).

· **autism**

A severe developmental illness that impairs the capacity to communicate and socialize.

· **post-traumatic stress disorder**

A disease characterized by failure to recuperate after experiencing or seEIng a frightening event.

Prevention

There are no sure means to stop the mental disease. But for those who might have a mental ailment, taking the time to restrain stress, to maximize your endurance also to boost low self-esteem might keep your symptoms in check. Follow the following steps:

· focus on indicators. Function with your health care provider or therapist to master that which could trigger your symptoms. Make an idea, so you know just what to do when symptoms come back. Get in touch with your physician or therapist if you become aware of any improvements in symptoms or the way you're feeling. Look at between relatives or friends to watch for indicators.

· get regular health attention. Do not neglect visits or jump visits to a healthcare provider, particularly if you are not feeling well. You could have a brand new health condition that has to be medicated, or you might be experiencing unwanted side effects of drugs.

· get assistance if you want it. Emotional health issues could be more difficult to cure should you wait until symptoms become worse. Long-term care therapy can also help prevent a relapse of symptoms.

· take decent care of yourself. Adequate sleep, wholesome eating and regular physical actions are crucial. Attempt to keep up a normal program. Speak to your main care provider when you have sleep disorders or if you have questions regarding diet and physical exercise.

Keep calm, the importance of control

Since early times, the individual philosophers have realized that the value of mind in regulating individual affairs. They knew a person's external situation was the consequence of their internal thoughts. These certainly were aware that in case anyone thought wealth, he'd be wealthy, as the notions of poverty, failure and success could create the corresponding effects from anyone's circumstances. Now, modern science has confessed the facts of those findings. Ergo it will become essential for an individual to restrain his brain.

Those dreadful unwanted thoughts. This hushed voice on the mind. Heart-pounding anxiety. Worried ideas that sew into terrifying scenarios. Terrifying dreams stuck on mind that won't disappear completely.

Negative ideas are somewhat disagreeable, frightful, and also the reason behind stress. They have also been that the destructor of a joyful life.

Now envision those notions - larger, stronger, and more rapid. That is what it seems like to someone with ADHD. Every idea is magnified, intensified, and amplified; rendering it not possible to work, or consider anyone and anything else.

Regardless of what your idea processing (ADHD or perhaps not) style is also, nobody escapes the curse of negative thinking. But it will have a beneficial side. (do not disappear, we will get to this shortly)

Mental poison sucks out the pleasure of one's day.

Negative thinking starts with 1-bit thought. It's a cause that causes an explosion, just like a very small pebble breaking away onto a snowy mountainside crumbling to an avalanche, tumbling out of hands. Superfast, you're buried under and cannot escape.

All evening

Sunlight does not cease the negativity. From the 3:00 knee shadow, you attempt to sleep soundly, but involuntary worries, anxieties, and terrifying dramas arise from the depths of one's subconscious mind. Such as a broken alarm clock you cannot shut off them.

Negative thoughts aren't any boundaries. Swirling away from one's hands, there's not any limit for thEIr barbarous cycle.

The best way to reclaim your thinking - negatively

Your primary line of protection is. The "diversion approach." a strategy utilized by parents of small kids. Frustrated and not able to avoid a crying child due to his favorite blankie was abandoned at the restaurant, so the parents even present a bright and glistening new thing to spend the youngster's attention away out of his despair.

Are you currently using the "diversion method" to neutralize yourself?

While I need to discontinue the bearing within my thoughts, the first thing that I do is grab something sweet. Relationships are my drug of preference. However, a part of chocolate or whatever sweet generally seems to take away my mind from those intruding, unwelcome thoughts. Strange, but true.

Are you currently a binge-watcher discovering assist sitting before this television all night watching zombies, politics, or perhaps the sword struggles in Westeros? Completely consumed, there's not any mental space to get one bad idea to input.

Sadly, some depressive behaviors become detrimental. It's simple to start overusing alcohol, drugs, food, video games, gaming, shopping, work, and yes the net. As a result of technology, we have to be independently together with all our obsessive minds.

Have you tried to cease your negative ideas eating a bag of chips or perhaps a spoonful of Talenti ice cream and soon you're feeling full, everything you can imagine is the way gross you are feeling? Which merely effects in feeling bad about yourself as you don't have any control over your impulses.

At the point, you're thus far removed from the initial bad idea; you cannot even remember what it had been. Yes! The diversion proved to be powerful.

The best way to reclaim your thinking - immediately

Negative ideas are valuable because they provide you with an opportunity to establish (to yourself) how strong you're. Gaining control within the mind is an energy skill that boosts your self-esteem.

Every evening is full of lots of chances to let negative believing principle your life and destroy your happiness.

Taking charge of your ideas is an art you must develop if you'd like a joyful life.

Negative ideas can't be ceased. But, you'll be able to get a handle on the length of time they stay on the mind.

You get a handle on your head. Now you decide as to exactly what you let in and that which you kick-out.

Mind-control is a personality power you want if you would like a reliable life.

There's a solution to divert your thoughts without enlarging your waist dimensions, feeling guilty, or looking at the television all day.

Some great benefits of mind-control: 5 good reasons why it's crucial to divert your thinking favorably.

1. You may feel like a superhero.

Emotional strength isn't allowing your thoughts go crazy. Nothing seems worse than slipping into the endless pit of emotional darkness. And nothing feels better than yanking out of this shadow, locating the lighting, and putting yourself to the trail to safety.

You may feel that a psychological superpower as if you've never believed before.

2. You'll have less battle

When negative ideas are not as dominant on the mind, you might be somewhat less bloated. Feeling calmer, you have got the capacity to disengage from the battle. Little matters fall right into perspective and also appear since they're little matters maybe not worth fighting.

Think about: why is that value my energy, time, and emotional wellbEIng? Conditions which can be crucial may be managed at a more efficient and respectful method.

3. You may sleep

It does not imply that the sacrifices and tumultuous dreams won't come. They'll. You cannot stop them. But- you can discover to discount them and get straight back to sleep, rather than turning and tossing into the shadow for three longer.

4. You'll be the master of your brain

Repeated behaviors (even quiet mental ones) become engrained on your subconscious mind. The longer you exercise gaining control over your head, the more, the longer it will become an integral part of you personally. Soon it'll be natural. When parting strikes and you also want to fight off it, your subconscious mind instinctively introduces the "positive diversion approach."

5. You may feel inner serenity

Emotional strength is understanding that you won't fall off as soon as the storm comes as well as your ship starts rocking. It's a feeling to be in control while staying strong and serene. Sounds fine.

Given you realize the advantages of controlling your unwanted thoughts, another website will teach you how you can take charge of one's mind — coming shortly!

But binge-watchers, please forgive me. I don't mean to defraud you. I only want to assist you in finding your inner strength and also taking charge of one's life.

Five reasons why staying calm under stress can allow you to be successful

You can find peaks and tours -- great days and bad days -- moods which arrive without the apparent motive.

There can also be much in mind, which frequently can cause overwhelm.

And we get off balance together with all our feelings swirling which contribute to bad lifestyle choices.

There's a lot of need — an excessive amount of participation, contrast, and grasping.

Folks seldom change off. You believe now assuming that you ought to be plugged.

People everywhere are so centered on texting or possess thEIr nose into your apparatus. I cannot believe the number of people I visit daily that need certainly to text whenever they have been still walking.

And also the noises of cities. Several people walk through incredible heights of noise pollution daily of thEIr metropolitan life.

Individuals that are capable of remaining calm under pressure tends to boost thEIr odds to be successful and accomplishing thEIr targets. Individuals who assert this serene mental outlook while in the midst of a hectic situation is able to view beyond the chaos in order to look for an option. As stated by research performed by talent smart, 90 percent of high actors on the job have a top eq or emotional intelligence quotient. Fifty-eight percent of our project performance is situated on our eq. Ostensibly our mental intelligence is how effective we're in acting and reacting maturely, in addition to our capacity to precisely process situation. Section of owning a top eq calls for our capacity to remain calm when under great pressure. This guide will address five good reasons staying calm in such situations is likely to make you successful.

1. You develop patience

One reason remaining calm under stress could cause you to be powerful is that you know to establish patience. For a prosperous practitioner, patience is vitally crucial in assisting one to efficiently manage emergencies and shine throughout all the barriers that can come your way. Consider the subsequent variable on what patience is manufactured through a stressful circumstance.

The genuine action of quitting to breathe greatly helps the human body to diminish its stress amount and alarms the human mind to know which you will need to decompress and settle down. Once you send the signal to the human mind, then alarms the remainder of your entire body to curl up. But if you're panicked and perhaps not calm, then your pulse and breathing increases and your blood pressure increases. These things can start to slow straight back to an ordinary pace while you start to calm your breath.

2. You develop optimism

Staying calm under stress may make you powerful since you develop confidence. With a positive prognosis is still another essential characteristic of an efficient leader. Successful men and women view the silver lining in every situation and recognize that confidence is a priceless part of them thEIr coworkers and employees to be successful.

Individuals who stay calm under pressure have realized that emphasizing positive things may enable them to ease stress while at negative scenarios. Within a stressful position, unwanted thoughts work toward boosting your stress level, which isn't great for your body or helpful for making effective decisions. Emphasizing positive thoughts will help in decreasing your stress level and keeping you far optimistic.

3. You eliminate negative self-talk

Still another reason staying calm could cause you to be powerful is that you eradicate unwanted self-talk from your life. If you look at powerful people today, they usually do not enable negative jellying to invade thEIr lifestyles. These folks have achieved their degree of success by emphasizing favorable self-talk is an invaluable way of penalizing them and their downline toward victory.

During stressful circumstances, individuals who stay calm can get rid of unwanted self-talk and concentrate on soothing their body through emphasizing favorable self-talk. They do not give attention to every one of the catastrophes which may occur but have not yet. They usually do not polarize everything and see each situation as either negative or positive. They understand just how to get the center-ground in equilibrium and situations the facts together with expectation for future alteration.

4. You build a positive mindset

Successful individuals have a positive mindset which divides them forward always to attempt to think beyond the package and seek out innovative methods to problems and issues at the workplace along with their businesses. Staying calm under pressure could cause you to be powerful as you build an optimistic mindset throughout your stressful adventures.

Successful men and women understand just how to remold their mentality so that the situations tend not to tear up them, but also make sure they are stronger individuals. They can manage destructive situations because they do not focus solely on what went wrong, but additionally attempt to obtain what went. They don't become victims of context but alternatively become victors in this very true reality.

5. You grow to be a team player

The last reason remaining calm throughout a stressful position could cause you to be powerful is that you develop into a team player. Being a team player and proficient at the craft of working with others and building a team is just one essential characteristic of an effective individual. Focusing on just how to efficiently connect to various sorts of people and help everyone relate well together might allow one to perform fantastic things on your workplace or business.

Many people don't run around like a chicken with no head in a catastrophe. Rather they have been focused and ready to quickly gauge the problem and ascertain the things they may do to effect positive change, and also exactly what they require aid in attaining. He or she then assigns emergency control steps to the others and help everybody make it throughout the stressful circumstance.

The best six advantages of becoming

You are feeling in charge of one's emotions and your life.

Increased breathing ability.

You're able to hear your thoughts.

Re-discover your creative stream.

You've got better communicating.

Love greater health.

However, how come being composed, therefore crucial that you perfect?

As the entire world becomes faster, we will need to slow down.

Adulting is tough work, and quite frequently no matter our great goals, positive vibes, life hacks, and excess vaporized gas for slaying our times

CHAPTER THREE

MANAGE STRESS AND MEDITATION TECHNIQUES
Stress control utilizing self-help processes for handling stress

It could look like there is not anything you can do about stress. The bills will not quit arriving, there'll never become hours daily, and also your job and household responsibilities will likely always be rough. However, you need much more control than you may think. In reality, the very simple understanding you are in charge of one's life may be your basis of tackling stress. Stress control is about accepting the charge: of one's way of life, emotions, thoughts, and also how you cope with issues. Irrespective of how stressful your daily life sounds, there are actions that you can take to ease the pressure and recover control.

Exactly why is it important to handle stress?

In case you are residing with large levels of anxiety, you are putting your whole wellbEIng in danger. Stress wreaks havoc upon your psychological balance, in addition to your physical wellness. It frees your power to think clearly, work effortlessly, and revel in life.

Effective stress direction, alternatively, can help you break the grip stress has in your lifetime, and that means that you may be happier, healthier, and more efficient. The ultimate objective will be that a balanced living, together with time for relationships, work, comfort, and pleasure --and also the endurance to maintain under pressure and meet challenges directly. But the stress direction isn't one-size-fits-all. This is exactly why it is vital to experiment to learn what is most effective for you personally. The subsequent stress management ideas may allow you to do so.

Tip 1: Identify the Sources of Anxiety on Your Life

Stress control begins with pinpointing the origins of stress on your life. This is simply not as straightforward as it sounds. As soon as it's simple to determine big stressors like changing jobs, moving, or even perhaps moving through a divorce, even differentiating the origins of chronic stress could be complicated. It's too easy to forget your thoughts, feelings, and behaviors promote your daily stress degrees. You might indeed know you are always focused on workouts, however maybe it's your procrastination, in place of the true job requirements, that's the reason for the strain.

To recognize the authentic sources of anxiety, look closely in your habits, attitude, and also explanations:

can you explain out stress as temporary ("I only have a thousand things going on now") while you cannot recall the last time you chose a breather?

Can you specify stress is an intrinsic part of one's job or home life ("matters are almost always mad around here") or like part of your personality ("I've plenty of nervous energy, so that is all")?

Can you blame your stress onto others or outside affairs, or visualize it entirely normal and unexceptional?

Before you accept liability for your role, you're in keeping or creating it, your stress level will stay out of your controller.

Tip two: exercise the four a's of anxiety administration

While anxiety is an automated response from the nervous system, a few stressors appear in predictable intervals: the commute into work, a meeting with your supervisor, or even family gatherings, such as. When tackling such foreseeable frustrations, it is possible to EIther alter the circumstance or change your reaction. When picking which option to select in any particular scenario, it's useful to think about these four a's: avert change, change, adjust, or accept.

Trick 3: obtain going

If you are worried, the last thing that you feel like doing is getting up and exercising. But physical exercise is an enormous stress reliever--and also you also don't need to become an athlete or even spend hours at a fitness center to go through the positive aspects. Exercise releases endorphins which make you feel well, plus it also can function as a very important diversion from the everyday stresses.

As you'll find the maximum benefit from frequently exercising for half an hour or longer, it's fine to develop your exercise level gradually. Even tiny activities may accumulate throughout the daily. The very first step is always to find yourself up and to move. Here are some easy ways to integrate exercise in your everyday program:

wear some songs and dancing around

have your puppy for a stroll

walk or bicycle into the supermarket shop

utilize the stairs in your work or home as opposed to an elevator

park your car in the right place from the lot and walk the rest of the manner

pair-up with a workout companion also promote each other as your workout

play an activity-based video match together with your children

Restore the Positive Mindset

Additionally, it is no surprise for you that positivity is, naturally, in the middle of psychology.

Positivity does not necessarily refer to only grinning and appearing cheerful, nevertheless --joy is much more about the entire outlook in life, and also thEIr inclination to concentrate on everything is good in everyday life.

In this bit, we will cover the basic principles of positivity within certain psychology, and identify several of the countless benefits of coming life from the certain perspective, and research some advice and methods for fostering a positive outlook.

Positive thinking is a psychological and psychological attitude that targets on the sunny side of life and also anticipates very good outcomes.

Favorable thinking means upcoming life's challenges with a positive prognosis. It generally does not of necessity mean ignoring or preventing the terrible things; as an alternative it involves making the most of the potentially awful scenarios, attempting to observe exactly the finest in different people, and seeing your abilities in a constructive light.

We can extrapolate from such definitions and also develop a fantastic outline of a favorable mindset while the inclination to concentrate on the bright side, expect favorable benefits, and approach challenges with a confident prognosis.

Having a favorable mindset signifies making sure believing a custom, always looking for that silver lining and making the most out of any situation that you end up in.

Traits and faculties of a constructive mindset: 6 cases

Thus, now we understand what a confident mindset is, we could dive in the upcoming major question: exactly what exactly does it resemble?

There are many attributes and traits related to a constructive mindset, for example:

optimism: a willingness to attempt and have an opportunity rather than imagining your efforts will not repay.

Acceptance: admitting that matters do not always prove the way you would like them, however, learning from their mistakes.

Resilience: bouncing back from hardship, disappointment, and collapse rather than quitting.

Gratitude: knowingly, always enjoying the nice stuff in your life (blank, 20 17).

consciousness/mindfulness: devoting your brain to conscious awareness and enhancing the capability to concentrate.

Integrity: the characteristic to be honest, righteous, and uncomplicated, alternatively of deceptive and self-explanatory (power of positivity, n.d.).

Perhaps not only are those faculties of a constructive mindset; however, they might also work from the other way --knowingly embracing confidence, acceptance, endurance, gratitude, self-indulgent, and ethics on your lifetime may assist you in developing and keeping a constructive mindset.

A-list of beneficial attitudes

Should you find that the list above too obscure, you can find a lot of more special cases of a confident attitude for actions.

To get example, positive perspectives may comprise:

it's looking hardship from the eye... And laughing.

Obtaining what you buy, rather than throwing a fit.

Appreciating the unexpected, even if it is maybe not exactly what you wanted originally.

Motivating people around you with a constructive note.

Working with the energy of a grin to undo the design of a circumstance.

Being favorable to people that you never understand.

it is getting back up once you collapse again. (regardless of how often you collapse)

fully is a supply of energy which lifts people around you.

Recognizing that connections are somewhat more important than things.

Being joyful even if you have little.

Exactly why is just an optimistic attitude considered the secret to success?

Today we understand slightly more in what an optimistic mindset resembles. We can turn into one of the primary questions of what's the deal with using a favorable attitude?

What is it all about using an optimistic mindset that's very important, therefore impactful, therefore life-changing?

Well, the faculties and faculties recorded above to provide us with a clue; if you comb throughout the literature, then you will observe various advantages connected to optimism, durability, and mindfulness.

You will see that consciousness and ethics are connected to enhance the caliber of life, and approval and gratitude usually takes you out of the "fine life" into the "good living "

The value of creating the proper thoughts

Developing a favorable mindset and acquiring all these benefits is a function of these notions that you nurture.

Do not worry --that this portion isn't about the type of positive believing that's all favorable, all of the time. We do not assert that only "believing happy thoughts" will bring you all of the success you would like in life, and we don't feel that confidence is justified in most circumstance, every single minute of this afternoon.

Developing the ideal thoughts is about being always happy or happy, and it isn't about dismissing anything unpleasant in your life. It's all about incorporating the favorable and damaging in your view and choosing to be generally positive.

It is about admitting you won't continually be happy along with learning how just to accept bad moods and hard feelings whenever they encounter.

Above all, it's all about increasing your hands on your personal attitude from the face of everything comes your way. You can't restrain your mood, and you also can't necessarily control the thoughts that pop into your face; however, you're able to choose the best way to handle these.

When you opt to devote to your negativity, pessimism, and also doom-and-gloom perspective of the earth, you're not simply submitting to your loss in control and also potentially wallowing in desperation --you might be passing up an essential chance for increase and development.

Based on favorable reinforcement Barbara Fredrickson, negative thinking, and unwanted feelings have their place; they let you sharpen your attention on risks, dangers, and vulnerabilities. That is essential for survival, but not up to it had been for the ancestors.

Construction a positive mindset for the thoughts is about bEIng annoyingly cheerful, however investing in your future. It's fine to feel do think sometimes pessimistically; however, choosing to react to confidence, endurance, and also gratitude will help you more in the long term.

Ten Advantages of a Positive Mental Attitude at Work

No construct better catches the gist of a confident attitude at work quite like emotional capital (or even psycap for short). This multi-component build is composed of four emotional tools:

hope

efficacy

resilience

optimism

Psycap was initially conceptualized as "positive emotional capital" by celebrated leadership and management investigators Luthans and Youssef at 2004. The idea immediately shot to popularity one of the favorable organizational founders, so that at 2011 there were hundreds of citations of both psycap from the literature.

The earliest meta-analysis of most the investigation on psycap was run in 2011, plus it outlined a number of the numerous advantages of psycap at the workplace:

psycap was favorably associated with project pride, organizational commitment, and emotional well bEIng.

psycap was positively associated with organizational citizenship (desired employee behaviors) and multiple measures of operation (self-rated, manager tests, and objective measures).

psycap was related to cynicism, turnover goals, job stress, and stress.

psycap was negatively associated with adverse employee deviance (lousy employee behaviors;

happier employees tend to be far more productive than other employees.

Joyful salespeople have greater earnings than other salespeople.

Joyful employees are far more creative than other employees.

Joyful employees are assessed more favorably by thEIr managers.

Joyful employees are not as inclined to reveal job withdrawal (absenteEIsm, employee turnover, job burn out, and retaliatory behaviors).

Joyful employees earn more income compared to other employees.

Overcome Social Anxiety

Lots of people get nervous or shy occasionally, such as when committing a language or preparing to get a new endeavor. But social stress disorder, or social anxiety, is significantly more than merely shyness or intermittent nerves. Social stress disorder involves intense anxiety about certain social situations--notably, situations which are unknown by that you believe you're being assessed or assessed by other people. These situations could be quite so terrifying for you to get anxious just considering these go to great lengths to prevent them disrupting your life in the approach.

How to conquer your social stress a cognitive behavioral therapy strategy.

If you discover yourself vaccinated and nervous in various social situations (speaking before a bunch, meeting new folks, with people lockers or break rooms, eating at people) and also you fear that folks are going to realize your stress and you will feel ashamed, and you might suffer from a social anxiety disorder. Lots of people who have this specific problem may opt to prevent situations where they expect being stressed, or they could use drugs or alcohol to self-medicate before inputting those situations. Social stress is linked with greater risk for alcohol misuse, depression, isolation, diminished occupational progress and the higher odds of staying single.

Underlying social stress disease may be the fear to be scrutinized, judged, or humiliated in people. You may well be fearful that people may think poorly of you or who you won't step up in contrast with others. And even although you probably recognize that the fears to be judged are somewhat absurd and overblown, it's still true that you cannot help feeling stressed. But irrespective of how painfully timid you are no matter how awful the butterflies, you're able to figure out how to become more comfortable in social conditions and recover your life.

The causes of social stress?

Though it may feel as though you are the only person with this particular issue, societal stress is very common. Lots of people have a problem with those anxieties. However, the situations which cause the signs and symptoms of social anxiety disorder could differ.

Some individuals encounter stress in the majority of social conditions. For many others, stress is attached to specific social circumstances, like talking with strangers, even furious at parties, or even acting before a viewer. Common societal stress triggers comprise:

meeting new folks

making little conversation

public talking

acting point

bEIng the middle of focus

bEIng observed while doing something

currently bEIng teased or criticized

discussing with "significant" individuals or jurisdiction amounts

currently bEIng called in course

moving on a date

discussing at a fulfilling

utilizing public restrooms

taking examinations

eating or drinking from public

making telephone calls

attending parties or other social events

Signs or symptoms of social anxiety disorder

Merely as you sporadically become nervous in social situations does not mean that you might have a social anxiety disorder or social anxiety. Lots of men and women feel shy or timid about an occasion, yet it will not get in the form of their regular operation. Social stress disorder, on the flip side, will not hinder your normal routine and causes enormous distress.

By way of example, it's flawlessly ordinary to find the jitters before giving a language. But in case you've got social anxiety, you may stress for weeks beforehand, call in sick to escape it or begin shaking so awful during the address you may barely talk.

Mental indications and signs of social anxiety disorder:

extortionate self-consciousness and stress in ordinary social situations

intense stress for days, months, weeks or months before an impending societal situation intense anxiety about bEIng judged or watched by other people, particularly people that you never understand

the stress you'll behave in a sense that'll embarrass or humiliate your self

stress that the others are going to observe that you are nervous

Physical symptoms and signs:

red confront or blushing

shortness of breath

upset stomach, nausea (i.e. Butterflies)

trembling or vibration (including rickety voice)

hemorrhagic heart or tightness in the chest

sweating or sexy flashes

feeling dizzy or faint

Behavioral signs and symptoms:

preventing social scenarios to a level that restricts your activities or interrupts your life

staying silent or concealing in the background to escape humiliation and notice a necessity to always bring a friend with you where you move

drinking before societal scenarios as a way to soothe your nerves

Social Stress Disorder in Kids

There is nothing unusual about a kid bEIng bashful, however, kids who have social anxiety disorder experience extreme distress within regular situations like using other children, reading in course, talking for adults, or even carrying evaluations. Many times, kids with social anxiety do not even wish to go to faculty.

The best way to conquer social stress disease suggestion inch: challenge negative ideas

While it may look like you'll find not anything you can do concerning the indicators of social anxiety disorder or social anxiety, the truth is, you'll find various things which could provide help. The very first thing is tough for your mindset.

Social pressure victims have negative ideas and beliefs which bring about their anxieties and stress. These may consist of notions such as:

"I know I will wind up looking just like a fool."

"my voice will begin shaking, and I will humiliate myself."

"folks will think I am dumb."

"I'll not have a thing to express. I'll seem boring."

Challenging these unwanted thoughts is an efficient means to lower the signs of social stress.

Measure 1: describe the automatic negative notions that encircle your concern with social circumstances. As an instance, if you should be worried about a coming job demonstration, the inherent negative idea may be: "I will dismiss it. Everyone will think I am utterly incompetent."

Measure two: analyze and challenge these ideas. It will help to think about questions in regards to the unwanted notions: "can I know without a doubt I'm going to dismiss off the demonstration?" or "even though I am worried, will people fundamentally think I am incompetent?" through this logical appraisal of one's unwanted thoughts, you're able to gradually replace them with more realistic and positive methods of studying societal circumstances which activate your anxiety.

Additionally, it can be incredibly frightening to consider why you believe and think how that you do; however, understanding the explanations for the anxieties will greatly lessen thEIr negative influence in your life. Unhelpful believing fashions which gas societal stress

Think about if you are engaging in someone of the next unhelpful thinking styles:

head reading -- assuming do you realize what other men and women are believing, they view you at exactly the exact unfavorable manner you view yourself.

Fortune notification -- predicting the near future, usually while supposing the worst may happen. You only "know" that matters will go horribly, which means that you're already worried before you are even at the circumstance.

Catastrophizing -- blowing things out of proportion. By way of instance, if people realize that you are worried, it is likely to be soon "awful", "terrible", or "devastating."

personalizing -- let's assume that people are working negatively or what's happening with different folks needs related to you personally.

Trick two: concentrate on the others, not yourself

Whenever we're at a societal situation which makes us many of us often have caught up within our anxious thoughts and feelings.

119

You may well be convinced that everybody is looking at you and judging you. Your focus is on your physiological senses, trusting that by paying extra close attention, you're able to control them. However, this surplus self-focus only makes you aware of just how nervous you are feeling, triggering more anxiety! Additionally, it prevents you from completely focusing on the talks around the operation you are giving.

Changing in the inner to outside attention can go a very long way towards reducing societal stress. It can be easier said than done; however, you cannot listen to just two things at the same time. The longer you consider what's happening around you, the less you'll be afflicted with stress.

Focus your attention on other folks --however, perhaps not about which they truly are considering you! As an alternative, do everything you can to engage them and also make a connection that is real.

Keep in mind that stress isn't as visible as you might believe. And if somebody finds you are worried, this does not necessarily mean they'll think poorly of you personally. The odds are different men and women are feeling as nervous as possible or did previously.

Tune in to what exactly will be said--to not your negative thoughts.

Give attention to the present instant, as opposed to fretting about what you are going to express or beating up yourself to get a flub that has passed.

Publish the pressure to be ideal. Rather, concentrate on bEIng attentive and genuine --qualities which other individuals would love.

Trick 3: learn how to control your breathing

Many modifications occur on your body should you get stressed. Among the initial changes is you start to breathe fast. Over-breathing (hyperventilation) melts the total amount of oxygen and carbon dioxide on the human body --contributing to more physical signs of stress, such as nausea, a sense of suffocation, higher heartbeat, and muscular strain.

Learning how to slow your exercising helps to bring your physical signs of stress under control. Assessing this breathing exercise can assist you to stay composed:

Sit together with your spine straight, and your shoulders relaxed. Put one hand in your chest and another in your tummy.

Stand gradually and deeply through your nose 4 minutes. The hands in your tummy need to grow, as the hands-on your chest should proceed very little.

Hold the breath for two minutes.

Exhale slowly via orally 6 minutes, pushing at much atmosphere as possible. The hands in your tummy need to proceed into because you exhale, however, your flip side needs to proceed very little. Continue to breathe through your nose and out through your mouth. Give attention to keeping a slow and stable breathing pattern of 4-in, 2-hold, and 6-out.

Trick 4: face your fears

Certainly, one of the very helpful things that you can do to overcome social stress is to handle the social situations that you panic as opposed to avoid them. Avoidance prevents societal stress from illness moving. While averting excruciating scenarios might allow you to feel better in the brief term, it keeps you from becoming much more comfortable in social conditions and learning how to deal ultimately. In reality, the further you avert dreaded social circumstances, the more frightening it's.

Avoidance also can stop you from doing things you may love to do reaching certain targets. By way of instance, a fear of talking can keep you from discussing your thoughts on the job standing outside in the classroom, or even making new friends.

While it might appear hopeless to overcome a dreaded social condition, you certainly can do it by carrying it one small step at one time. The crucial thing is, to begin with, a predicament which you're able to handle and gently work your way around harder scenarios, building your confidence and working skills while you proceed up the "pressure crate."

By way of example, if interacting with strangers leaves you stressed, you may start with accompanying an incoming friend into an event. Once you are familiar with this measure, you may decide to try introducing yourself to a new individual, etc. To operate your way upward a societal stress ladder:

Do not attempt to confront your main fear straight away. It is not a fantastic idea to proceed too fast, take on a long time, or induce matters. This can backfire and fortify your anxiety.

Be patient. Overcoming social stress takes practice and time. It's gradual, incremental progress.

Make use of the abilities you've discovered to remain composed, such as concentrating on your breathing and hard unfavorable assumptions.

Socially getting together with co-workers: an example pressure ladder

Measure 1: say "hi" into co-workers.

Measure two: ask co-workers questions about the way to accomplish tasks on the job.

Measure 3: ask a co-worker exactly what they did the weekend.

Measure 4: sit from the team area through coffee-break.

Measure 5: eat dinner in the team room.

Measure 6: eat dinner at the team room and make little conversation to colleagues (e.g., discuss the weather, sports, current events, etc..)

Measure 7: ask a co-worker to choose coffee later work.

Measure 8: venture outside for lunch with a bunch of co-workers.

Measure 9: share private information about yourself with co-workers.

Measure 10: attend a team party.

Suggestion 5: create an effort to be social

Earnestly looking for supportive social surroundings is just another effective method of hard your anxieties and overcoming social stress. These hints are great ways to begin interacting with other people in positive manners:

Require a societal skills course or an assertiveness training class. These classes are frequently offered in local adult education centers or community colleges.

Volunteer doing something that you like, like walking dogs at a refuge, or pruning for an effort --something which may provide you with an action to concentrate on as you're also engaging with a few like-minded men and women.

Focus on your communication abilities. Great relationships are determined by clear, emotionally-intelligent communicating. If you discover you might have trouble linking to the others, learning the fundamental skills of emotional intelligence might help.

Strategies for earning buddies even if you're shy or socially embarrassing

However awkward or nervous you believe in the business of many others, you may learn how to silence self-critical ideas, and boost your self-esteem, and also eventually become more confident and more secure on your interactions with other individuals. That you do not need to modify your personality. Simply by learning new abilities and embracing another perspective, you can overcome your fears and stress and also build rewarding relationships.

Trick 6: adopt an anti-anxiety way of life

The brain and the body will be closely connected --and a growing number of evidence implies the way to treat the body could have a substantial impact in your stress levels, your ability to handle stress symptoms, and also your general self-confidence.

While lifestyle modifications alone are not sufficient to overcome social anxiety or social anxiety disorder, they could encourage your total treatment advancement. This lifestyle recommendation can assist you to decrease your general stress levels and also set the platform for successful therapy.

Avoid or restrict caffeine -- coffee, soda, tea, and energy drinks become stimulants which increase stress symptoms. Look at cutting caffEIne out altogether, or even keeping your intake limited and low into your afternoon.

Get busy -- create physical activity a priority --30minutes daily whenever at all possible. Should you hate to exercise, consider pairing it with something that you do like, such as window shopping while walking laps around the mall or dance to your favorite music.

Insert more omega3 fats into a diet plan -- omega3 fats encourage brain health insurance and may enhance your mood, prognosis, and also capacity to take care of stress. The very best sources include oily fish (salmon, mackerel, herring, mackerel, anchovies, sardines), seaweed, flaxseed, and walnuts).

Drink just in moderation -- you could be tempted to drink before a societal problem to calm your nerves; however, alcohol increases your probability of experiencing a stress attack.

Cease smoking -- nicotine is a strong stimulant. In contrast to public opinion, smoking contributes to higher, not lower, rates of stress. If you will need help kicking the habit, visit: how to stop smoking.

Get sufficient quality sleep -- if you are sleep deprived, you are prone to stress. Being well-rested will assist you to keep calm in social scenarios.

Social Stress Disorder Therapy
In case you have attempted the self-help technIQues over, and you are still fighting with disabling social stress, you might need expert assistance too.

Therapy for societal stress

Of all of the professional treatments available, cognitive behavioral therapy (cbt) has been demonstrated to work well for treating social anxiety disease. Cbt is founded upon the assumption that what you think affects the way you're feeling, and also your emotions impact your behavior. Therefore, in the event that you change how you believe of societal scenarios that provide you stress, you're feeling and work better.

Cbt for social anxiety might involve:

Learning the way to get a handle on the physiological signs of stress through relaxation methods and breathing exercises.

Challenging negative, unhelpful thoughts which activate and gas societal stress, substituting them with more balanced perspectives.

Facing the societal situations, you dread at a slow, orderly way, as opposed to avoiding them.

As you can understand and practice those exercises by yourself, if you have had trouble using self-improvement, you can gain from the additional guidance and support a therapist attracts.

Role-playing, social skills instruction, along with other cbt methods, frequently as a member of a treatment team. Group therapy uses behaving, videotaping and celebrating, mock interviews, along with different exercises to focus on situations which make you stressed in the actual world. As you exercise and prepare yourself for situations you are fearful of, you also will end up increasingly convenient, as well as your anxiety will decrease.

Drug for Social Anxiety Disorder

Medication is occasionally used to ease the signs of social stress; however, it isn't just a cure. Medication can be recognized as very useful when used, along with therapy and self-explanatory methods that address the main cause of one's social stress disease.

Three forms of drugs are employed in treating social stress:

Beta-blockers are utilized for alleviating performance stress. While they don't impact the emotional signs of stress, they could restrain physical symptoms like shaking voice or hands, perspiration, and rapid heartbeat.

Antidepressants can be useful when societal stress disease is intense and debilitating.

Benzodiazepines are fast-acting anti-anxiety medications. But they're sedating and addictive, and are on average prescribed only when other medications have worked.

BUILDING RELATIONSHIPS
What's relationship-building about?

Relationships would be the blocks for all community organizing tasks. Whether you wish to arrange a volleyball match or eliminate unfair housing practices in town, you'll need plenty of good connections. Why? As the connections we have with your colleagues, the communities we all serve, and also our adversaries would be the way for achieving our targets. People do not work in isolation: we all will need to be operating together! It's our relationships all included together, which can be the base of an organized attempt for the shift. We require a lot of individuals to donate their thoughts, have a stand, and find the job done.

It's also the individuals that motivate us to accomplish goals. As community contractors, we care deeply about caring and people a part of our job. It's our looking after the others which pushes us to operate too as we all perform. It's frequently the joy and health of our kids, nEIghbors, and colleagues we possess fixed in our heads even as we push ourselves to overcome barriers and undertake challenges which could feel overwhelming.

If you're the state chief or an active citizen with a formal name, you may soon be effective if you set many strong relationships on your at the area.

In this section, we'll discuss the construction and keeping relationships and provide you with some practical methods and overall instructions.

And recall: average men and women understand the abilities to establish and keeping connections all of the time. That you never have to be especially enchanting, witty, or even talented. But if you have been enchanting, witty, or even talented, these recommendations can help you, too!

Fundamental reasons to build relationships:

Community construction happens one-to-one. You want to create relationships with all individuals one-of-a-kind if you desire them to become involved in your group or company eventually. Many folks participate in associations because they have confidence in the reason. But a lot of men and women get involved at a community group or company, simply as they will have a romance with yet another man or woman who's already engaged.

We want relationships as a way to win allies to your origin. To be able to find support from those out our associations, we will need to create relationships by which people understand and trust.

Our connections provide richness and significance to our job as well as your lives. Most of us want a network of individuals to talk about the joys and the struggles of coordinating and making network change. Just a small amount of camaraderie goes quite a ways.

What Types Of Relationships Are We Talking About?

Every connection differs, however all of the issues. If you grin and say hello into the school crossing guard in the best approach to work daily, you've formed a romance. That crossing shield might be the person who'll be watching for the children or grandchildren when they're mature enough to walk into school on thEIr own. The shield will remember you along with your hot grin when calms your kid throughout the street. And the crossing shield is going to function as the main one which you finally recruit to venture up the taxpayers' traffic security committee.

Your connection with all the crossing guard might be somewhat distinct from the connections that you have with people involved with your local park-cleaning committee. The connections that you have with the mayor's aide, even with your team, together with members of one's board of supervisors, along with your better half will be different, but all of them play a significant part in community organizing.

The more connections you have, the better. You will never know if they should arrive in handy. A nEIghborhood gang member may be just the man you want to assist you in organizing a set to create a brand new park on your area. Whether they have been government officials, school educators, people, grandparents, anglers, kids, people with disabilities, displaced people or individuals else--construction friendships will probably pay off in ways you might not ever have anticipated.

You're at the middle

Imagine a wheel where you're in the heart or center, and each talked reflects a connection with someone else. Does sound egocentric? It will not have to become. It will take a whole lot of spokes to contain the wheel together and also the wheel is what helps to move the initiative together. There's sufficient space in the category for all to produce thEIr particular wheel of strong relationships.

The purpose is that you must take the time to prepare and preserve relationships. If you wait around for other people to ascertain relationships with you, you might devote plenty of time.

One reminder: it does not make sense to sort relationships to make folks accomplish to meet your needs. That won't work as people will feel well used. Community contractors approach relationships with integrity. We form connections because we truly like somebody, because we've got something to offer which person, or as we share some frequent objective.

When Do You Build and Sustain Relationships?

You get it done all of the time. Should you choose an additional five minutes to ask the individual who's stuffing envelopes the way they think the baseball team will be achieving this calendar year, you may have assembled a stronger relationship.

Some associations need additional time compared to others. You might choose to meet for lunch monthly, including the rest of the supervisors of youth businesses in town. You might want to generally meet two weekly with a team member with any developed bitterness about the project. You might choose to telephone your faculty committee representative every occasionally to test in concerning topics of concern.

As neighborhood organizers with a couple of resources, we're frequently under enormous pressures which divert us from focusing on relationships. We believe that the urgency of achieving major targets. We wrongly believe hanging out relationships would be your fluffy material which makes someone feel well, but does not get the business finished. Many times, nevertheless, relationships are the secret to solving an issue or obtaining the occupation. Assembling and sustaining most solid, strong connections is fundamental to our job as leaders.

Relationships are the Groundwork

Usually, building relationships is your groundwork that has to be placed before whatever else has done on a job. The greater the job, the more connections you'll often want as a base.

For instance, if you're organizing a coalition of community groups who may function to generate a multicultural arts center, it'd have been a fantastic idea to become familiar with people in each company before looking to purchase them together to focus with the undertaking.

Consider: "can you're persuaded by somebody who you know, or with an entire stranger?" afterwards be advised by your answer.

If you want a job, you want to include the time that it takes to create relationships in your plan. Folks need time to construct trust. Whenever people interact, they will need to trusting relationships. If confidence is lost, people normally have a challenging time functioning cooperatively. They fret about risking a lot. Disagreements appear to erupt without a major reason. Purchasing resources, and also something's organizational standing can be insecure. At minimum men and women need some return to thEIr financial commitment. They need to feel as if you understand them like an individual, know thEIr interests, and also won't permit them down.

Straight back into the multicultural arts center case in point -- when creating one will demand several community classes, of course, if you do not understand them well (plus so they don't know each other), take effect together to a bigger job. As an instance, you're able to sponsor a day of cultural sharing collectively. If the day is powerful, you may have gained some confidence and trust where to build. You're able to plan a few similar events which may build trust over some time.

If matters aren't moving well back upward and attempt a simpler challenge. If you start to put on discussions on the multicultural arts center, and also people reveal signs of apprehension as opposed to the excitement, then slow the procedure. Take on a simpler challenge until strong connections are better based.

Establish relationships before you want them

It is always better to construct relationships earlier; you want them before a conflict arises. If you currently have a fantastic relationship with all the food storeowner on your area, you're going to be soon able to position to help solve a dicey battle between him along with some locality adolescents. For those who have already created a connection with your faculty committee agent, then she is readier to reply to your remarks about special education financing.

Establishing Relationships in An Emergency

It's not impossible to launch relationships during a catastrophe, and many times a catastrophe may bring people together. While it might look odd, take advantage of your business's crises. Telephone for assistance and also people can climb into your telephone. You're able to construct connections whenever you're in serious need, as we frequently desire to provide help.

How will you build relationships? An 11-step method

Here are a few tips for getting the relationships from the soil. A number of those ideas we heard at the initial tier nevertheless, as adults, we sometimes forget about.

Build relationships one at any given period. Luckily or regrettably, there aren't any shortcuts. Distributing a newsletter assists you stay in contact with a lot of folks, but there isn't any replacement to get to understand a true individual.

Make friendly and earn an association. This might appear self-evident; however, an agreeable smile or word can make some one's day. Look for something in common: we all wish to have intimate connections with all our fellow humans.

Ask folks questions. People today want to talk about themselves and around what they believe. Should you ask people about themselves and take a moment to listen carefully, they are your buddy.

Tell people about yourself. Individuals will not expect you until you are eager to anticipate them. Tell them everything you care for and what you believe.

Proceed places and do matters. If asked why he robbed banks, then the robber responded, "because that is where the money is." if you would like to make buddies, you must go where the individuals are: picnics, conventions, events, parties, parties, playgrounds, bowling alleys, little league games, bake sales, etc..

Accept people the direction that they truly are. You do not need to concur with them constantly to produce a romantic relationship together. Nobody likes to be judged.

Assume additional men and women wish to make connections, too. Under that, the crabbiest looking man is frequently a lonely soul trusting someone will make a fracture into their shell.

Overcome your fear of rejection. The majority of us suffer from panic of rejection, and there is just one thing to do relating to this: get it over. In case you wish to make relationships, intend on bEIng refused a number of this moment. You'll be richly rewarded the rest of times together with all the newest connections you've made.

Make constant. Individuals are usually shy and questionable. It requires a while to acquire confidence. You can typically form a connection if you adhere together with it.

Invite visitors to join up. People today wish to become a part of something larger than those eventually. A lot of people are searching for an opportunity to meet different men and women who share common targets. At the worst, most folks will likely be flattered you encouraged them to combine.

Love people. If you truly like people, the others will probably be drawn to your mindset. Individuals will probably desire to be around one.

CHAPTER FOUR

HOW DO YOU BUILD RELATIONSHIPS WITH PEOPLE OF DIFFERENT CULTURAL BACKGROUNDS THAN YOUR OWN?

Below are some basic recommendations:

learn concerning the individual's civilization. Any attempt will go a long way in demonstrating you care enough to figure out about the reality of some other individual's life.

Set yourself in the middle of some other individual's civilization . Especially if you're dealing with understand somebody who's maybe not just a part of majority civilization, consider visiting thEIr ethnic events at which you stand the minority. If you're eager to take risks and put yourself at a position where you are feeling uneasy, folks will soon be more prone to desire to get to understand you.

Require a stand contrary to anyone's oppression. Actions talk louder than words. Individuals who undergo oppression want allies to speak out against chaos. Strong relationships have been forged once folks act courageously concerning every other.

It is okay to make mistakes. You might need to create mistakes since you build relationships with individuals that have different ethnic backgrounds in the personal; however, people are often forgiving, particularly if your goals are good. Bear in mind, hang in there if you're feeling rejected.

How will you build relationships with people who hold positions of political ability?

Here are some tips for forming connections with elected officials, industry leaders, and even heads of large associations.

Do not hesitate. Individuals who hold positions or titles of governmental authority are all humans, too. They prefer to create connections as everybody can.

Forged and withhold judgment. People who have names rarely find a chance to be paid attention to. They rarely find an opportunity to think through a problem without someone forcing them to vote one way or the other. 1 way to forgive this kind of a man is always to take enough time to obey them. See what you're able to offer them not in a political circumstance but as a sympathetic individual.

How Will You Sustain Relationships?

Ok, now you have assembled some relationships. Relationships, like any living thing, want care to keep them healthy and alive. Therefore what exactly do you do using them to continue to keep them moving?

Pay focus on individuals. Checking with folks when you want to. This can take just several minutes every week, but those few moments will make the distinction in assisting your buddy or co-worker remember the significance of the job you're carrying out together.

Admits publicly. People today will need to convey. It's a fantastic idea to reserve a while to discuss how things are moving. If people have an opportunity to discuss major problems, mistakes can happen and anxieties frequently buildup. Communication can be a subject which needs to be practiced regularly; it's like taking vitamins or doing push-ups.

Love every other. Everybody else has to be valued to be able to continue to keep relationships going. If you realize that someone did a stellar job of collecting the vital information to your committee, then state. If you love dealing together with somebody else, make them understand. We're all people and admiration helps us flourish.

Stretch yourself. Move a bit from one's way, at least one time every so often. If your co-worker should devote a little additional time together with his daughter, then you may let him proceed home early, and you're going to wind off the award proposal.

Volunteer to accomplish some job to their company (in case they're not already in yours). If you give them a hand, then they will likely believe good of you personally and give back something in exchange.

Challenge one another to accomplish better. Most of us want a friend to help us beyond what we think we may perform. We may even build stronger connections with hard our job spouses to carry on bigger challenges.

Straight back each other when things get rough. Loyalty is necessary for keeping relationships healthy. We might well not trust a co-worker or friend; however, we can uphold her or him once they have a jam.

Acquiring buddies

Friendships are more valuable than simply sharing laughs within a cup of java. A scarcity of strong relationships increases your probability of premature death from all causes by 50 percent, based on research by Harvard University. That is the very same mortality risk as smoking 15 cigarettes each day. If a societal life is appearing light, it may be the time to create some new friends; however, it generally does not need to be an embarrassing and embarrassing procedure.

The secret to making new friends can be as easy to be receptive to it. Listed below are six things that you can do to fulfil your calendar and devise new friendships:

Twenty- and - 30-somethings are one of the very "social" people out there. With this kind of energetic presence on societal networking, they will have constant opportunities to talk about the minutiae of the everyday lifestyles with hundreds of thousands or hundreds of thousands of individuals.

Yet at precisely the same time, there is a great reason to trust American adults tend to be lonelier than ever before. An analysis of over 1,700 19 - to 32-year-olds discovered that frequent social networking users were three times more likely to feel isolated.

Plus, studies reveal that those digital connections are not almost as pleasing as the in-person kind. Could it be maybe time that you put only a tiny bit of additional effort into a face friending? You may discover your happiness quotient slipping up when you're doing.

Forging new friendships or strengthening older ones isn't always simple, so below are a few hints which are somewhat more creative and more practical compared to the older " put out yourself."

The best way to create new friends

1. Carry on a buddy

The majority of us have heard about this "blind date," that the thought of letting a pal play matchmaker and put us up with someone we've never met.

In case you've only moved to your different town, have a friend put you on an entirely free date together with a few of these friends who reside nearby. You should have less to lose in case the possible game will not workout.

2. Be authentic

It is time to receive super clear about which you like to complete. As you pursue hobbies and activities you like, you get a fantastic probability of meeting people who have similar interests.

Assess out that neighborhood lecture on modern literature or sign to get a sushi-making class. Each event can be an opportunity to meet an entire roomful of likeminded friends.

You can additionally volunteer your time and ability with a non-profit that resonates with you or download meet-up to get local folks who have similar interests. Of course if you fail to locate the group you'd like, why don't you start one? Just a tiny vulnerability could result in lifelong relationships.

3. Get up-close and private

Creating a close relationship does take some time. Fourteen days, in reality, according to a 2018 study.

When you're only beginning to become familiar with someone, cultivate familiarity by discussing something deeper than the sucky weather. Gradually disclose something purposeful on your and see whether your brand new friend is going to perform the very same.

Should you want fodder, all you might answer the question "should you can wake up tomorrow having gained any one caliber or skill, what could it be?" this technIQue could perhaps you have bonded very quickly.

4. Be consistent

Even though perhaps not all of us have got the guts to accomplish it, the majority folks understand how exactly to pursue a beat. Swipe right. Send flowers with your workplace. Invite them to your concert in a group you realize they'll love. Ask them to test "yes" or "no more" under the question "are you going to go out with me" on paper.

Oh, wait... Are we not in third-tier anymore?

Employ similar (but less amorous) approaches when chasing a possible friend. By way of instance, send the man a message requesting them to coffee or lunch a week, and follow-up then to express you had a fantastic time plus cite something special which has been memorable or funny.

5. Decide on a target

It could sound shallow; however, next time you visit an event, tell you to wish to leave together with three brand new friends (or perhaps one).

This manner, you're going to become open to meeting people and starting a detailed conversation instead of merely grinning at the individual before you in line for your restroom.

6. Say cheese

Seriously. We're including grinning with this list as it is a far more potent strategy in making relations than you may believe. To begin with, grinning goes out of one's head and cause you to think more about the image you are projecting.

plus 2015 analysis found when designing new connections; individuals are somewhat more receptive to positive emotions compared to emotions such as sadness and anger. In other words, you are more inclined to contact someone whenever you talk about a smiley moment compared to the usual one. So carry on, show off those white teeth.

7. Do not take it

We pretty much understand what this means when an enchanting partner tells us "it is not you, it's me" but when you encourage a brand-new pal to java or some pictures, and so they turn you down, then do not panic.

Maybe they are busy with labor. Maybe thEIr relatives take up an excessive amount of time. Consider it is not you. Perhaps you can take a raincheck and decide to try again later on.

8. Think outside the box

It is potential that until now, all of your friends are 20-something women who are employed in fashion. However, why limit yourself? Variety may be the spice your and that.

Now you might just as easily hit it off by someone twenty years older than you who works in the fund. Be amenable to forming new connections using co-workers, nEIghbors, and classmates, and however distinctive out of you that they seem to become.

The way to maintain old buddies

They have seen us weep on the passing of our goldfish and laugh so hard our gut is sore the following time. However, given that all of us are "professionals," it's easy to become swept up in the delight of new social circles and also forget about our older pals.

The hints below can assist you in maintaining those twists strong by bEIng fair, unobtrusive, and inviting.

149

1. Take it easy

Thus, Sara forgot your final birthday and mark never left it into a holiday party. As hurtful because thEIr seeming lack of attention may be, try to lower your older pals some idle.

As an alternative of supposing they are becoming mean or do not worry of your relationship, consider they are overrun by family or work responsibilities (also bear in mind that you've probably experienced precisely the same ship sometimes).

2. Discuss the facts

There is nothing such as a pal who can let it to you directly. If a buddy asks you a problem in regards to a new project or dating, attempt to become as receptive as you possibly can. You'll construct a feeling of confidence, along with your friend, will likely be prone to encounter with honesty regarding your lifetime.

3. Be nearly current

Even although social websites cannot substitute for real friendships, then face-book is a fantastic way to seek out old buddies and strengthen old ties if you participate.

Pairing overall status upgrades ("only ate breakfast! Delish") does not do much for intimate relationships. But posting on somebody's wall to direct them getting into grad school could be quite meaningful.

4. Keep it short

A lot of us have now been around in this example: " we recEIve a contact from an old pal and defer answering it before we now have the full time and attention span of publishing a novel-length answer (i.e. Rather than).

An improved plan would be to ship frequent, short mails therefore that you remain in the loop around one another's lives rather than go a long time without an upgrade.

5. Put it on newspaper

By the time we come home from a long day of errands and work, we may have little energy left to get a catchup session. However, if there is an "appointment" about the calendar, then we still cannot miss it.

Schedule standard calls or dinner dates together with pals who live a long way away -- there is a fantastic chance you're going to be pleased you did not bypass it!

6. Proceed with the stream

If a friend experiences a major change, like moving to another city, marriage, or even with a kid, your partnership together is likely to improve, too.

As an alternative of stressing that matters won't ever be the direction that they used to (but cannot we remain all evening drinking wine and talking the significance of life?), give attention to what you need in normal today.

Be supportive of one's friend's brand new life. Bear in mind, they are probably still the same individual, only with a bit more life experience.

7. Be busy together with your friend

Say you two accustomed to going together weekly; however, you've not been connected for a yr. Rather than establishing a potentially embarrassing java date to reconnect, indicate hitting on the bowling alley enjoy in the previous times.

It will provide you with an opportunity to renew your friendship while doing something that you enjoy. It is also going to eliminate some of its pressure to create small conversation.

8. Get out of city

Research suggests that encounters can make us happier than actual products. And what better adventure is that there than spending with a set of close friends?

If a friend goes away, think about saving to get a small road trip to see and go out into thEIr brand new ground. Likewise, let your friend know that your sofa is always offered.

9. Try out a program

In case you've transferred a long way away from the previous network, not worry -- there is a program for this, ostensibly such as the lovechild of snap chat and Facebook messenger.

There is a good voice filter to produce you seem as if you inhale helium, in the event, you feel inclined. The creative possibilities with the program make long-distance relations superb fun.

Why we want friends

Boffins have understood that humans are social animals, wired to gain from intimate relationships with relatives, romantic partners, and needless to say, friends.

A watershed 1988 study discovered that folks who have the fewest social relations had a general higher chance of dying compared to individuals who have purposeful connections.

What is the offer? Research shows that social isolation increases cortisol (stress hormone) levels inside our bodies. This may cause inflammation, lack of sleep, and also hereditary changes -- all risk factors for chronic diseases and sooner departure.

As though this was not sufficient to convince one to look for a best friend, a summary of 19 studies found that social isolation can be connected with dementia.

The take-away

Sometimes it merely happens -- we all bond on a mutual love of harry potter or acquaintances, and next thing we all know, we're fulfilling for a week brunch.

However, other times it is tougher, and also, we cannot help feeling as though we're the only real man at the party with no partner in crime.

Anything the conditions, it is crucial that you stay at it rather than get frustrated. Together with enough self-confidence, flexibility, and patience, so it is possible to obtain friends in just about any problem -- and maintain them.

CHAPTER FIVE

HOW TO ANALYZE PEOPLE

The spot to begin would be to ask, "why to analyze this individual?" the demand for an investigation usually directs the sort of investigation that's conducted. If a man or woman is obtaining a work afterwards, one pair of procedures have been used. If emotional disruption is under consideration, afterwards, another pair of procedures have been used.

Given that people have the "why" question replied, we can move. For today I shall assume that the individual has requested work. Which exactly are the individual's advantages? Which is going to be the next matter soon. No matter how the clear answer will frequently be dependent on which strengths are wanted for this particular circumstance. This too, we're often constrained by the requirements of this examination. If direction skills are crucial, I am taking a look at matters just like "dominance" and "sociability."

I want to consider the flaws this person brings to this career. Exactly what exactly are the traits which will hamper the individual's performance? Where would they drop onto these matters as "impulsive" and "physical and social stress-prone."

An overall, omnibus stock is useful as it frequently highlights characteristics and issues which weren't initially believed. In this way that an investigation usually begins with a screening to its typical general faculties and also screening to psychopathology.

Most clinical psychologists have contributed a lot of ways you may test people.

1. Create a base-line

Folks have various quirks and patterns of behavior. By way of instance, they may clean their neck, examine the floor while talking, cross thEIr arms, then scrape thEIr thoughts, stroke thEIr throat, squint, pout, or jiggle their toes usually. Initially, we might well not even see if others do all these things. When we do, then we still do not give it much interest.

Folks exhibit these behaviors for various factors. They can only be mannerisms. Sometimes, on the other hand, the very same actions might be indicative of ignorance, anger, depression or anxiety.

2. Search for deviations

Pay focus into inconsistencies between your baseline you've established and anyone's gestures and words.

As an instance: you've realized an essential supplier of yours gets got the habit of clearing his throat when worried. Since he presents some relatively tiny modifications to your small business arrangement, he starts to achieve that. Can there be more than meets the eye?

You may opt to research farther, asking a couple more questions than you'd normally have.

3. Notice clusters of expressions

No single gesture or phrase inevitably means anything, however, if a few behavioral aberrations are clumped together, bear note.

For instance, not only does your provider keep draining his throat, but, he makes this mind scratching item. And he keeps shuffling his toes. Proceed with caution.

4. Compare and comparison

Okay, so you have discovered that somebody is behaving somewhat different than usual. Move up your observation a notch to determine whether so when that individual reproduces the same behavior together on your group.

Keep on observing the individual as she or he disagrees with the others inside the space. Is it true that the individual's saying change? How about her or his position and body gestures?

5. Look into the mirror

Mirror neurons are built monitors within our brain, which represent other people's condition of mind. We're wired to see the other person's body gestures. A grin activates the grin inside our faces, even though it triggers our tight muscles.

When we see somebody we enjoy, our eyebrow arch, facial nerves relax, mind-boggling, and blood flows into our lips which makes them fuller.

In case your spouse does not provoke this behavior, this individual might be sending you a crystal-clear message: she or he does not like you or are not pleased with whatever you've done.

6. Identify the strong voice

The most powerful person isn't always the only sitting at the pinnacle of this desk.

Confident people have powerful voices. Around a seminar room table, probably the confident man is quite possible to be one of the most successful one: grand position, strong voice, and a significant grin. (do not confuse a loud voice using a strong one)

If you are offering a concept to friends, it's simple to look closely at this pioneer of the team. But that pioneer could have a poor personality. He or she is based heavily on the others to make conclusions, and it is readily influenced by these.

Identify the strong voice, as well as your odds for success, increase considerably.

7. Detect they walk

Often, individuals who shuffle together, insufficient a flowing motion inside thEIr moves, or maintain their head lack self-confidence.

If you notice those traits at a part of your group, you could make an excess effort to offer commendation, in an endeavor to help build the individual's confidence. Or you might have to ask her or him direct questions within a gathering, as a way to pull those fantastic thoughts out in the open.

Bases of gestures

Body-language identifies to the nonverbal signs we use to convey. According to experts, these non-verbal signals compose a massive portion of everyday communication. From our decorative expressions into our entire body motions, what we do not state can nevertheless communicate amounts of advice.

1. It's been implied that the body language could account for between 60 percent to 65% of communication.

2. knowing body language is significant, but it's also essential to listen to other cues like circumstance.

Often, you ought to check at signs as an organization as opposed to emphasizing a single action.

Here is what to keep an eye out for if you are attempting to translate gestures.

Facial expressions

Consider a second how much a man or woman can communicate with only a facial expression. A grin can signify happiness or approval. A frown indicates disapproval or even disputes. Sometimes, our facial expressions can disclose our true beliefs in regards to a specific circumstance. Even though you say that you're feeling alright, the appearance in that person can tell people differently.

Only a couple of examples of feelings which can be expressed through facial expressions comprise:

happiness

sadness

anger

sur-prise

disgust

stress

con fusion

excitement

want

contempt

The term on an individual's face may help ascertain whether we hope or believe exactly what the average person says. One study discovered that probably the trustworthy facial manifestation involved a small raise of the eyebrows and a small grin. This saying, the investigators implied that communicates both friendliness and optimism

Research also suggests we make conclusions about people's intellect based upon their expressions and faces. One analysis found that individuals who'd more slender faces along with more prominent noses were far somewhat more likely to become regarded as apt. People who have to grin, happy expression were also judged to be apter than people who have mad expressions.

The eyes

The eyes are often called the "windows into the soul" given that they can handle showing a whole lot about exactly what a man or woman is feeling or believing. Since you take part in a dialogue with someone else, bEIng attentive to eye motions is an all-natural and significant part of the communicating procedure. Some common points you might notice include whether they're making direct eye contact or preventing thEIr disposition, how much they're blinking, or when thEIr students are dilated.

When assessing body-language, focus on this next eye signs:

eye thought: whenever an individual appears into your eyes while using a dialogue, it indicates they are interested in and attending to. But, prolonged eye contact may feel threatening. On the flip side, breaking eye contact and usually looking away could demonstrate that the man or woman has been diverted, uncomfortable, or even seeking to hide their real feelings.

Blinking: blinking is not natural; however, it's also wise to listen to if someone is trapping too much or inadequate. Folks frequently float faster once they're feeling stressed or uneasy. Infrequent blinking might signify a person is blatantly attempting to restrain thEIr attention motions.7 as an instance a poker player may float less often because he's trying to seem unexcited on the hand that he had been dealt with

Pupil size: pupil size might become described as a rather subtle non-verbal communication signal. While moderate levels from the surroundings get a grip on student dilation, occasionally feelings may also result in modest fluctuations in pupil size. As an instance, you might have heard the term "bedroom eyes" used to describe the appearance someone gives once they're drawn to some other individual. Highly dilated eyes, as an instance, can indicate a man is curious and sometimes maybe stimulated.

The mouth

Mouth expressions and expressions are also important in studying human anatomy language. By way of instance, chewing over the bottom lip can demonstrate that the particular person is experiencing feelings of stress, fear, or unhappiness.

Within the mouth might be an attempt to be considerate if the man or woman is coughing or coughing; however, it might also be an effort to cover a frown disapproval. Smiling is maybe among the best human body language signs; however, smiles are also translated in a variety of ways. A grin may be real. Also, it could be utilized to express false joy, sarcasm, or perhaps cynicism.9

When assessing body speech, focus on this next month and lip signs:

pursed lips: tightening your lips may be a sign of distaste, disapproval, or doubt.

Lip biting: individuals sometimes bite thEIr lips once they're stressed, anxious, or worried.

Seal the mouth: whenever folks desire to cover up a psychological reaction, they may pay their mouths to prevent displaying smiles or smirks.

Pops dor up: minor changes from your mouth may be subtle signs of exactly what a man or woman is the atmosphere. After the mouth is slightly turned out, it may signify that the man is feeling optimistic or happy. On the flip side, a marginally down-turned mouth may be a sign of despair, disapproval, and an outright grimace.

Gestures

Gestures can be a number of thEIr very direct and clear body-language signals. Waving, pointing, and with all the fingers to signify numerical numbers are all common and simple to comprehend gestures. Some expressions might be cultural, but therefore giving a thumb up or perhaps a peace hint in still another country may have a very different meaning than it can in the USA.

These examples are only a few frequent gestures as well as thEIr potential significance:

A clenched fist can signify anger in a few situations or solidarity with others.

A thumbs up and thumbs dare usually used as expressions of acceptance and disapproval.10

the "fine" gesture, created by touching along the thumb and index finger in a ring while also stretching another three palms may be used to imply "fine" or "all " in certain areas of Europe; nevertheless, the same signal can be employed to imply you're nothing. In a few South American nations, the emblem is a primitive gesture.

The V-sign, created by raising the index and middle finger and then dividing them to generate a V-shape, means peace or success in certain nations. At the UK and Australia, the emblem assumes an offensive significance once the rear of the hands is facing externally.

The legs and arms

The legs and arms may help communicate non-verbal info. Crossing the arms may signal defensiveness. Crossing legs far from the other individual could signify distress or dislike with this particular person.

Other subtle signs like enlarging the arms broadly might be an effort to seem bigger or even more controlling while keeping the arms near your human body could possibly be an endeavor to minimize oneself withdraw out of attention.

When you're assessing body-language, listen to a number of those following signs that the arms and thighs can communicate:

Crossed arms may indicate an individual feels strange, self-protective, or closed-off. Reputation with hands set on the buttocks might be an indicator a man is willing, and in hands or also, it can potentially be an indication of aggressiveness.

Clasping the hands behind the trunk may signal that a man or woman is feeling exhausted, stressed, as well as mad.

Immediately tapping palms or fidgeting may be an indication that a man or woman has been tired, tired frustrated.

Crossed thighs can signify that a man or woman is feeling shut off or needing solitude.

Posture

The way we grip our bodies may also function as an equally significant part of human body gestures. The expression position identifies the way we hold our bodies in addition to the general physiological kind of somebody. Posture can communicate an abundance of details regarding just how a man or woman is feeling and tips on personality traits, like if someone is certain, receptive, or even person.

Sitting upright, by way of instance, might indicate an individual has been focused and making time for what's happening. Dealing with your system hunched forwards, on the flip side, may mean that the man or woman is tired or indifferent.

When you're trying to learn gestures, make an effort to observe a few of the signs, an individual's position could send.

Open position includes keeping the back of their human body exposed and open. Such a posture indicates goodwill, openness, and openness.

Closed posture involves concealing the back of their human body regularly by hunching forward and keeping the legs and arms crossed. Such a posture is a sign of hopelessness, unfriendliness, as well as also anxiety.

Did you ever hear somebody refer to their requirement for private distance? Have you begun to feel uneasy whenever someone stands a touch too near you?

The expression proxemics, chased by anthropologist Edward T. Hall describes the length between people because they socialize. As human body movements and facial expressions may convey a fantastic deal of non-verbal info, therefore can this bodily distance between humans.

Personal space

Four degrees of social space that occur in various scenarios:

Intimate distance-- 6 to 18 inches: this degree of physical space frequently indicates a closer relationship or increased relaxation between individuals. It normally occurs during intimate contact like hugging, whispering, or even touching.

Private space -- 1.5 to 4 feet: physical distance in this degree usually occurs between those that are household or close family members. The closer that the individuals can comfortably endure while socializing may be a sign of the degree of familiarity in their association.

Social space – 4 to 12 feet: this degree of physical space can be used with folks that are acquaintances. With somebody who you know quite well like, for instance, a co-worker you visit a few times weekly, you are feeling comfortable interacting at a distance. In scenarios where you don't know your partner well, like a delivery driver, you see once monthly, a space of 10 to 12 feet will feel convenient.

Public space -- 12 to 25 feet: physical space in this degree is commonly utilized in speaking in public situations. Discussing in front of the class filled with students or even giving a demonstration in the office are illustrations of such scenarios.

It's also very important to note that the amount of personal space that individuals will need to feel comfortable might differ from culture to society. One oft-cited illustration may be that the gap between people from African American cultures and individuals from united states. People from Latin nations tend to feel much more comfortable position nearer to the other person since they socialize while people from united states desire more personal space.

Recognizing gestures may go a long way toward helping you communicate with the others and understanding exactly others may be looking to communicate.

While it might be tempting to select besides signs one, it is crucial to check at such non-verbal signs regarding verbal communication, additional non-verbal signs, and also the circumstance. It is possible to even concentrate on learning about the way to enhance your non-verbal communication to be much better in letting people know exactly what it is you might be feeling--without saying a word.

What's NLP (Neuro-Linguistic Programming)

Neuro-linguistic programming is a method of shifting some one's thoughts and behaviors to help achieve desirable consequences for them.

The prevalence of programming or NLP is now widespread as it started from the 1970s. Its applications include treatment of migraines and stress disorders and advancement in workplace operation or individual happiness.

NLP is the practice of knowing how folks organize thEIr believing, feeling, speech and behavior to generate the outcomes they perform. NLP provides individuals who have a methodology to simulate outstanding performances attained by geniuses and leaders within thEIr area. NLP is additionally used for private development and also for success in business

An integral section of NLP is that individuals create our exceptional internal mental maps of this world for an item of how we filter and also comprehend information consumed through our five senses by the world around us.

What's NLP?

NLP can be utilized for individual development, nervousness, and stress.

NLP utilizes behavioral, behavioral, and communication tactics to produce it a lot easier for folks to change thEIr thoughts and activities.

NLP depends upon terminology processing but shouldn't be confused with natural language processing, but that shares the same acronym.

NLP has been developed by Richard Bandler and john grinder, who believed it had been possible to spot the different routines of thoughts and behaviors of powerful individuals and also to instruct them to other folks.

Just how does this function?

The varying interpretations of NLP help it become tough to specify. It's based on the thought that folks operate by internal "channels" of their world they know through sensory adventures.

NLP tries to discover and alter unconscious biases or limits of a person's map of the earth.

NLP is perhaps not hypnotherapy. On the contrary, it works throughout the mindful use of speech to result in changes in some one's mind and behavior.

To get example, a fundamental quality of NLP could be the thought that a man has been biased towards a sensory apparatus, referred to as preferred representational system or prs.

Therapists can find that taste through speech. Phrases such as "I see your point" could indicate a visual prs. Or "I hear that your purpose" could indicate an auditory prs.

An NLP attorney will determine an individual's prs and base thEIr curative frame around it. The frame may involve rapport-building, information gathering, and goal-setting together with them.

Methods

NLP is a broad area of exercise. Therefore, NLP professionals utilize many diverse methods that include these:

One of the methods of NLP would be to make an effort to get rid of negative ideas and feelings associated with an earlier event.

• **anchoring:** engaging sensory adventures directly into activates for several psychological conditions.

• **rapport:** the professional tunes in to anyone by fitting thEIr physiological behaviors to boost response and communication during compassion.

• **swish pattern:** modifying patterns of behavior or idea to arrive at a desirable alternatively of an undesirable outcome.

• **visual/kinesthetic dissociation (vkd):** attempting to eliminate destructive thoughts and feelings related to an earlier event.

NLP Origins

Neuro-linguistic-programming started its life in the 1970s in which an associate professor from the University of California, Santa Cruz, john grinder, awakened having an undergraduate Richard Bandler. Both men had a desire for individual excellence that charted a course for them to mimic behavioral patterns of selected geniuses.

Modelling could be your center task in NLP, also is your procedure of extricating and copying the speech architecture and behavioral routines of an individual who's exemplary at a specified activity.

Grinder and Bandler began their NLP pursuit by simulating three individuals, Fritz Perls, Virginia Satir and Milton Erickson. All these geniuses were outstanding as professional representatives of change, employed in the domain of therapy. All three geniuses, Perls, Satir and Erickson played their magical in the perspective of subconscious excellence. The geniuses failed to introduce grinder and Bandler using an aware description of this behavior. The modelers (grinder and Bandler) unconsciously consumed the patterning inherent from the geniuses after which give a description.

With little direct awareness about every one of those genius's specialty and little understanding of the area of psychotherapy overall, grinder and Bandler within two years layout with excitement bordering on fervor, to explicate selected elements of their geniuses' behavior. They coded the consequences of these job from language-based variations employing the routines of grammatical grammar while the descriptive language. Throughout NLP modelling grinder and Bandler made explicit that the tacit skills of this geniuses and also NLP was firstborn.

The business that grinder and Bandler were keeping in such heady days of the 1970s has been a melting-pot of enquiring minds searching research into individual behavior. John grinder has been an associate professor at the University of California, Santa Cruz and Richard Bandler, a fourth-year undergraduate student. The entire world-renowned anthropologist Gregory Bateson had joined the college in Kresge college; also this was Bateson's curiosity about grinder and Bandler's alliance he introduced grinder and Bandler into Milton Erickson. Bateson given support, his excitement is in part recorded within his introduction to the publication layout of magic at which he says, "john Grinder and Richard Bandler did something very similar to that which my coworkers and I first attempted fifteen decades back."

Back in 1975 grinder and Bandler presented the initial two NLP models on the planet from the volumes "construction of magic I and ii." the amounts released by the esteemed publishing house "science and behavior books inc" placed NLP on the interest and map from the brand-new area of NLP propagate fast. People in areas associated with communication, behavior and shift hunted to learn just how they too can easily get incredible results when doing shift work. Grinder and Bandler voluntarily offered courses from the use of their models. The practice classes Bandler and grinder ran - established that the NLP units had been transferable to the others, meaning that the students might make use of the NLP models successfully within their work.

NLP Modelling, NLP Training, NLP Application

Where NLP started its existence as a method of filming excellence, courses soon became an extremely busy portion of the NLP experience, accompanied closely by NLP application where NLP trained men and women employ thEIr NLP programs for personal and commercial benefit.

NLP modelling

NLP modelling is your craft of earning explicit the collection of differences present in somebody who's exemplary at a certain activity wEIghed against somebody who's fair at exactly the same activity. NLP modelling is most certainly the maximum skill level in NLP. NLP modelling enables you to catch patterns of excellence contained in anybody in virtually any circumstance.

Most businesses within the NLP community put no or little accent on modelling. Michael Carroll attended an NLP route straight back in 1995 and has been frustrated the trainer publicly admitted he 'did not know a lot about modelling'. After Michael put the NLP academy, he guaranteed to model are an essential portion of this NLP academy doctrine. Modelling is a significant quality of our master practitioner course. Modelling can be featured from the NLPedia master practitioner study set.

Throughout the years, john grinder has continued to build up his skills as a modeler. He stands head and shoulders over the remainder of the field for a man or woman who can catch the routines of excellence inherent in virtually any outstanding individual. John grinder, together with his partner Carmen Bostic St Clair, offer filming training together with all the NLP academy.

NLP Training

After the NLP programmers started to discuss thEIr understanding, NLP accreditation became available together with different coaches. Ten years following the NLP beginning, contemporary day NLP training will come in several sizes and shapes, some great, good quality, plenty of ordinaries plus some decidedly inferior. At the NLP Academy, we have been pleased with our training listing. The standard of NLP academy practitioners and master practitioners speaks volumes to our job.

NLP application

An NLP practitioner could use thEIr abilities within a representative of change working with people, groups, or businesses, and sometimes even worldwide organizations as well as authorities. As a tech, NLP comes with a remarkable history for the fastest quick and efficient shift in groups and individuals.

A lot of people study NLP to assist them to be much more efficient within thEIr preferred field. The routines can be used across a broad range of software which ranges from subjects as diverse as education, team building events, sales, promotion, personal development and direction and training. Wherever there are human interaction and growth potential, NLP is employed to improve and improve performance.

Top 5 NLP tactics that will transform your life

1. Dissociation

Maybe you have been in a scenario which gave you a terrible impression? Perhaps you have undergone something that gets you every single time you go through it. Or maybe you get anxious at some job situations in which you need to speak openly. Perhaps you get bashful once you want to approach that "someone special" you've had your eye. When these feelings of sadness, anxiety or anxiety are seemingly automatic or un-stoppable, NLP methods of dissociation may help tremendously.

describe the emotion (e.g. Fear, anger, disquiet (dislike of a predicament) you would like to knock out

envision you could float from your body and return on your own, limiting the full circumstance in the observer's perspective

observe that the atmosphere affects radically

for the additional boost, imagine you could float from your body appearing on your own, subsequently, float out with the human body, so you are taking a look on your own, appearing on your own. This dual dissociation ought to take the unwanted emotion away just about any minor problem

2. Content re-framing

Try out this procedure once you feel that a circumstance is helpless or negative. Re-framing will need some unwanted circumstance and also enable you by altering the significance of this experience into something positive.

By way of example, let us state that the dating ends. This might appear bad in the top, but let us reframe it. Exactly what will be the probable added benefits to be unmarried? As an instance, you are open to additional prospective connections. You might also need the freedom to accomplish exactly what you desire, whenever you would like. And also you've learned invaluable lessons out of this relationship which will permit one to possess better connections later on.

These are all cases of re-framing a situation. By reframing the significance of this breakup, you provide yourself with another connection with this.

In anticipated scenarios, it is natural to fear or concentrate on panic, but that leads to more issues. By comparison, altering your attention from the manner just described enables you to clean your thoughts and create responsible, even-handed decisions.

3. Anchoring your self

Anchoring appears with Russian laboratory Ivan Pavlov who attempted dogs ringing a bell while the dogs were still eating. After repeated bands of the shot, he discovered that he could find the dogs to salivate by ringing the bell even though there is no food gift.

This generated a neurological association between the bell and also the behavior of jelqing knas a conditioned reaction.

You can use these types of stimulus-response "anchors" yourself!

Anchoring your self enables you to associate any desirable positive psychological reaction with a specific term or sensation. Whenever you select a beneficial emotion or idea and deliberately join it to your very simple gesture, then you also can activate this anchor any moment you are feeling low, along with your feelings will instantly change.

describe exactly what you would like to texture (e.g. Confidence, enjoyment, calmness, etc..)

decide where you want to position this anchor onto your entire body, like pulling your ear lobe, touching your knuckle or squeezing out a fingernail. This physical signature will let you activate the positive impression at will. It isn't important where you select, so long as it's an exceptional touch you never touch for whatever.

Think about a period before once you believed that condition (e.g., optimism). Mentally return into this point and float in your entire body, appearing through your eyes and reliving your particular memory. Correct your body gestures to coincide with the memory and also thEIr condition. See exactly what you saw, hear what you heard and believe that the atmosphere as you understand that memory. You'll start to believe this condition. That is comparable to telling your friend a funny story by earlier times as you "enter into" the story, you begin to laugh since you "associate" into the narrative and "relive" it.

Since you return straight back to the memory, then touch/pull/squeeze the area in the human body that you chose. You may truly feel that the atmosphere swell as you refresh the memory card. Publish the signature that the moment the emotional condition peaks and starts to burn. This will produce a neuro-logical stimulus-response that'll activate thEIr condition when you earn that touch. To feel that condition (e.g., jealousy), only touch yourself the same manner again.

To produce the answer much stronger, think about the other memory at which you believed that condition, return and relive it on your eyes, also anchor thEIr country on precisely the same area as before. Whenever you put in the following memory, then the backbone grows livelier and certainly will activate a stronger response. Utilize this system whenever you want to modify your mood.

4. Getting others to like you (rapport)

This is a simple pair of NLP methods, but they possess the capacity that will assist you to obtain together with practically anybody. There are tons of techniques to build a relationship with someone else. Certainly one of the quickest and most effective ways originates out of NLP. This system involves subtly mirroring the other individual's gestures, words.

People like those who are enjoying themselves. By subtly mirroring one other individual, the brain fires away "mirror neurons," pleasure detectors from the mind, making people feel a feeling of liking for anybody mirroring them.

The method is straightforward: stand or stand how the other man is still sitting. Tilt your face exactly the exact same manner. Smile if they grin. Mirror thEIr face expression. Cross your thighs whenever they blend off thEIrs. Mirror thEIr voice, etc.

The key to making a subconscious rapport is subtlety. If you're just too overt, each other might notice knowingly, that may likely violate rapport. Keep your mirroring calm and natural.

5. Influence and persuasion

Even though much of the job of NLP is dedicated to helping people expel unwanted emotions, limiting beliefs, bad customs, battle and more, still another portion of NLP is specialized in just how to influence and convince the others.

One of those mentors from the area was a man called Milton h. Erickson. Erickson was a psychologist who studied the subconscious head through hypnosis (the real, scientific material. Perhaps not the ridiculous amusement hypnosis you see at period shows).

Erickson was adept at hypnosis, " he developed a means to consult with the subconscious minds of different folks without having misuse. He can hypnotize people everywhere, anywhere in regular conversations. This Ericksonian procedure of communicating became famous as "conversational hypnosis."

This is a strong tool that may be utilized not just to influence and convince the others but also to help other men and women overcome fears, limiting beliefs, battle and more with thEIr conscious comprehension. That is particularly useful when getting across to individuals who may otherwise be watertight if they understand (think adolescent kids who do not desire to listen).

Ten tools to re-code your behavior

Do you fight with overcoming bad habits? Do you think it is tough to stay to a fitness routine constantly wind up right back where you started?

In case thus, what do you imagine if I told you could isolate your mind and break bad habits very similar to the way the computer developer programs signal? Sounds crazy? Yet, it's maybe not.

Much like to programming code, it's likely to reprogram deeply ingrained customs. Computer programming is an ideal metaphor for hacking, writing, or minding our very directions. We see that if we compare computer programming into custom formation.

What we all understand from laboratory studies is the fact that it is never too late to violate a custom. Habits are malleable throughout your whole life. But we know that the simplest way to improve a custom is to know its arrangement -- which as soon as you tell people concerning the cue and also the payoff and you also induce them to comprehend what those facets have been in behavior, it gets much, a lot simpler to improve.

Thus just what is computer programming, custom formation, and also how do we reprogram our profoundly ingrained customs?

What's the coding?

Coding is a completed pair of guidelines referred to as a schedule. We have to compose code in a particular manner for this app to get the job done. In nature, we must write code at a language where a computer can comprehend. Several computer languages exist, for example like HTML-5, CSS, c, c++, python, and JavaScript.

Think of our life as a finished pair of directions. To be able to reprogram it, we must write our code in a means that'll affect our bad habits. Essentially, we have to locate a reward system that our body and mind can move to.

Computer code is comparable to individual DNA; also, it functions exactly as the code within the computer program. Juan Enriquez educates us

Sequencing DNA decodes its programmatic goals through its connection to a blend of 4 letters of the alphabet: a, c, t, and g.

DNA is a self-replicating material contained in most living lifeforms and conveys our genetic details. Tom bunzel shows that the similarities within his publication DNA are pc software, who "wrote" this code? By setting a bronchial genetic code side-by-side using a hypertext markup language (HTML), that's the code to get a website page.

Design is a metaphor for writing directions for a lifetime

My purpose here isn't to ask who or that which composed our life code (and sometimes even how it's done). I would aim to demonstrate computer programming language (code) is a metaphor for life. The personal computer application is our life, where the personal code is our customs.

We can change our customs and switch off genes and forth through epigenetics. We are aware that contemporary geneticists can modify genes on / off with DNA internal applications. Essentially they have been copying and pasting code.

Moreover, programming is composing directions for computers, the place where a final group of directions is a laptop application. Life is just the same. As programming is composing directions for a personal computer, our everyday activities and customs are writing directions for a lifetime. Understanding how to code will make an improved computer application, therefore why don't you learn your code to construct a better?

Coding (habit-breaking) directions

We locate the signal or activate notifying our mind to go into automatic style. Secondly, we identify that the regular, that's the behavior itself. Third, we recognize that the benefit, that's what which produces our brain remember the "custom loop" at the foreseeable future.

Measure 1: describe the regular

Much like knowing the arrangement and aspects of computer code, so it's necessary that individuals must first realize the different elements of our loop.

Measure two: try out benefits

We utilize specific inputs once we code, therefore why don't you alter the inputs to find out if we obtain another output. In the same way, a pal attempted his benefit by adjusting his regular see whether it'd deliver another sort of reward. By way of instance, rather than walking into the cafeteria that, he walked across the cube.

Measure 3: isolate the cue

We can inquire (and listing our replies) five matters that the minute an impulse hit us to diagnose our dependence. These questions are fundamental to hacking on our code (customs).

Which are you?

What's it?

What is your psychological condition?

Who is around?

What actions preceded the impulse?

Measure 4: take a strategy

Locate a clear dependence. As we find our "habit loop" we can alter our behavior. That resembles the rewriting code.

We can re-program or hack on code (customs) by knowingly making decisions. We do so by making plans and also a fantastic way to that is by way of implementation goals.

If-then strategy

An "if-then" strategy is not any different than computer terminology. In the event you compose a code, even then you'll find an output signal.

This is where the computer programming // individual life metaphor creates the most sense if you ask me personally. By way of instance, let us first imagine people have been created as a sterile smartphone.

Today let's imagine two distinct baits to get a sprite or image on the phone (symbolizing us). This picture reflects two chances for our lifetime. We may grow to be a healthier and fit person, or people may grow to be an obese and miserable individual.

We must learn how to write or code guidelines to turn into the fit and healthy individual. Essentially, we must figure out how to reprogram (or hint) our entire life.

We can write directions for the finished schedule (our life). I've identified specific guidelines coded for my lifetime at the image below. These directions may be envisioned as customs.

Let us check a number of those bigger blocks of code I've assembled (where the outcome has established a strong and fit person): dawn, nutrition, exercise, water, comprehension, instruction, family, spirituality, along with occupation.

Essentially, if we after morning, we may then jump take up a wholesome morning workout.

If we exercise, eat and moisturize, we may then appear and feel great.

If we try and increase our wisdom and experience an intimate relationship with your loved ones, then we can live a happy and healthier life.

Managing Your Brain

Managing mind and feelings aren't easy once you go in the world. You are worried about every single day obligations as well as the'drama-rama' which occurs in the whole world. As a way to adjust your life, it is going to induce you to oversee your emotions and mind. Figuring out the negative on your life, also concentrate on the favorable. Quit hanging out with those who suck the life out of you personally! This may be tricky when they truly are friends and family. , the family could be the hardest since we're taught that family is equally crucial. However, how essential could it be? Isn't your wellbEIng essential? Unless you have your health, you won't be in a position to look after your loved ones. It's something to consider.

Approaches to handle your mind and your feelings produce a fantastic workplace.

There was nothing much more dispiriting than appearing at where you're likely to examine and finding it satisfies you with all gloom. Try and maintain a specific location, an area or section of space, for the work. Ensure this place attractive on your way. Decorate it with images, or flowers, or anything its which you like. Make yourself an inviting dining table, for instance, by eliminating unnecessary mess.

· **list the actions ahead.**

We often tend to use some other excuse to not return to work, plus yet one is doubt over where you can begin "shall I try so, or so?" and the doubt becomes a justification for doing something different. Plan exactly what it is you're likely to do the job on. The easy method of writing a set of the several what to complete and the sequence in that you're getting to get them may save a lot of wasted moment. Do your best not to be overly rough once you create your plan. You may always do something extra by the end in case there's still time.

· maintain the advantages definitely at heart.

Nevertheless easy you make it yourself to initiate the task, there'll nonetheless be a little hump to conquer. You want to keep until you the huge benefits to be gained by doing the job. With large tasks that can be especially essential; differently, a first enthusiasm could wane, and you will not ever discover the ability to begin. Write all of the stuff you might profit out of working on the project, and also read the list whenever you're due to the beginning, to provide a boost. That is very beneficial when you're going through a few of these stages whenever you are feeling frustrated or have missed the heart.

· leave workplace enticing for the next moment.

Many folks clean up, to obtain what that they want as a way to start, at the start of the workout. Once they block the session, they leave everything at a cluttered mess. The issue with it is the jumble becomes a hurdle to starting the subsequent workout. The remedy is straightforward. Spend the final few moments of this analysis span tidying up and planning for the following semester, so it will soon be simple to begin. Additionally, this is certainly one of the better times to plan what direction to go.

· **our people.**

That is challenging in regards to the family. How do you sing out of your spouse/partner? Concentrate on the good within these. Find something that they do this makes your heart soar and give attention to this. If it involves co-workers or perhaps a boss, give attention to this. They are only your boss or co-workers. You utilize them, and that is it. They truly are not aside from the inner circle (a number of them could be); they are only people that you find daily in your work. Locate the great in these. They could have more issues than you personally. Send them plenty of love and thank god you don't have thEIr problems!

· **cease and notice your thinking.** Gradually, see that your thoughts. Exactly what exactly are you believing? Might it be authentic? How could it be helping or hindering you? If you always think unwanted thoughts, your life may reveal your thoughts. Consider the folks in your life. Have a look at the situations which can be attracted for you. Are they negative or positive? It is likely that they truly are negative and maybe not healthy. Once you see your thinking, you're going to be in a position to alter them.

· **once you observe a negative idea, then alter it.** If you become aware of that, a 'negative' notion etched into your head, then alter it. Say, "thanks for discussing" and allow it to go through your thoughts. Do not provide it with some attention. Say, "that is interesting" and allow it to move. Do not stop to live or test the notion. Should you do, you won't stop, and you're going to draw more mental poison for your requirements personally.

• **move outside in character.** Contrary to popular belief, nature will be able to allow you to. Opt for a walk at the park or forests. If you reside within a place which has mountain parks, then go for an increase. Nature may work amazing things for the head, body, and soul. Imagine everyone the 'icky' energy in mind starting the ground. It is likely to be soon transmuted to love.

• **meditate.** This can be simple for a lot of as you want to sit for ten or more moments. Take to five full minutes every day and develop from there. Allow your mind to ramble and do not stop to test your thoughts. Notice them and allow them to go. Before you realize it, you will have to meditate all night! If you require assistance with meditation, then purchase a meditation cd or publication. It'll shift your ideas and life.

Overcome Depression Through NLP

Do not worry, be joyful, remain calm - you can find an infinite number of daily expressions that encourage us to become stress-free. However, in today's busy, busy universe having all these demands on our time and numerous responsibilities, it's sometimes tough to perform.

We confront possibly stressful situations every single day, from reflective interactions in the office to stressed scenarios inside our lives.

21st-century stressors can take several diverse types, from information overload and electronic offences to contradictory priorities, financial stresses as well as, very often, the pressures of forcing our complicated and congested roads. Unresolved problems; matters people opt to dismiss, exude or skirt round, may also fester and show themselves in stress, stress and depression.

Sometimes we could cope with those stressful situations without a detrimental effect on our emotional wellbEIng. And there's also such a thing as positive stress', which we frequently used at a job position or even to spur us during a job. But issues can arise if stress becomes negative (if we believe we cannot handle it).

It throws off our balance, influencing our wellness insurance and wellbEIng and most facets of our lives. When stress is lengthy, it could cause problems around duration and quality of sleep, wEIght gain, gastrointestinal issues and lots of different symptoms. On average, stress might be damaging to one's center, affect memory and may also lead to havoc with your relationships. Stress, tension and depression are closely correlated and usually interlinked and could form into physical sadness if left unattended.

As stated by stress UK, 40 percent of incapacity worldwide arrives at depression as well as stress.

Statistics reveal that, at Britain, 6 million individuals are influenced (approximately 3 million together with melancholy and 3 million together with stress). This astonishingly large statistic reflects nearly 10 percent of the general population of the United Kingdom. Nevertheless, the fantastic thing is that there exists a lot you can do to prevent, manage and fix stress, stress and depression.

Neuro-linguistic programming (NLP) will enable us to discover and understand that the main causes of stress, stress and depression and identify changes which have to be made. It might be anything from handling anxieties and anxieties and unwanted beliefs to solving problems by the past or worries about the near future.

Dealing with having an NLP coach will let you truly arrive at the underside of inherent problems so you can manage your life more resourcefully and proceed forward. Valuable NLP methods can introduce you to new methods of believing, which then, provides balance to your life.

If stress, anxiety or melancholy is something that you have trouble with, try out this advice to get you back on course:

Exercise and physical exercise

Proven to enhance mood and boost nitric at the system, transferring the body can benefit your emotional health in addition to your physical wellness.

Routine sleeping pattern

Keeping into a routine sleep routine - and - making sure you're getting enough sleep nightly - may diminish adverse feelings and stress.

Be cautious

Oodles of study demonstrates mindful actions might help with stress and melancholy. When it's mindful, opting for a walk in the atmosphere another sort of self-care, all these may very persist following a very long moment.

Yoga

Well-known for reducing and preventing anxiety from the near future and short-term, yoga, Pilates or tai chi may make a time out inside our busy schedules. You might try out a set training or class on your home with the guidance of an internet video.

Meditation

This could be an extremely powerful way to gain management of bodily strain to discover inner peace.

Comfort

Do calm the emotions and clean your brain. OverwEIght people are more inventive and may solve problems more readily, seEIng matters from another perspective.

Stop and ask

In case a stressful idea happens, first inquire if it's accurate. When it's not, let it move and if it's, think about perhaps the idea is effective? From here, you may choose a technIQue to take care of this.

Write it d

Take note of matters which are bothering you. Frequently, when you actively tackle issues, investigate problems and research solutions - it may assist by itself. If daily issues are you, look at putting aside a particular period once you can think of these. This manner, you can restate, so you can get on with your life for another day.

CONCLUSION

The activities we produce within our life are all largely according to our emotions and emotional intelligence. It makes sense that when people have a fantastic awareness of organizational and communication abilities, they'll soon result in possessing the capability to make proper decisions and interactions with other individuals. What we know from our emotions can let us pursue living style we would like to live and make more of what we desire within our lives, in the place of that which we don't. Emotional intelligence is a feature which may continually be nurtured and augmented in but with an improved awareness of this, the individuals will deficiency adoring friendships, internal enjoyment and broadly speaking be relegated into living a lifetime of non-social function. Becoming more conscious of the differences and impacts of eq and IQ frequently makes us think that eq is satisfactorily more significant compared to one's overall intellect because bEIng authentic to oneself could be the simplest means of living life to the fullest. In this international era, it's crucial to compile a good sense of psychological consciousness. After all, who wishes to live a miserable life with not having the ability to share everything with usually the person we love?

CPSIA information can be obtained
at www.ICGtesting.com
Printed in the USA
BVHW041400011220
594599BV00015B/1510